THE
LANGUAGE
OF
DOORS

PAULO VICENTE AND TOM CONNOR

THE

LANGUAGE

OF

DOORS

ENTRANCEWAYS FROM COLONIAL TO ART DECO

HOW TO IDENTIFY AND ADAPT THEM TO YOUR HOME

ARTISAN

New York

Published by Artisan
A Division of Workman Publishing, Inc.
708 Broadway
New York, New York 10003-9555
www.artisanbooks.com

Library of Congress Cataloging-in-Publication Data
Vicente, Paulo.
 The language of doors : entranceways from colonial to art deco : how to
identify and adapt them to your home / Paulo Vicente and Tom Connor.
  ISBN-13: 978-157965-2722 • ISBN-10: 1-57965-272-7
   p. cm.
  1. Doorways. 2. Architecture, Domestic—United States.
  I. Connor, Tom. II. Title.

 NA3010.V53 2005
 721'.822—dc22

                                    2004062262

Printed in Italy

10 9 8 7 6 5 4 3 2 1

Book design by Mauseth Design, LLC

To my beloved wife and companion
for holding down the fort, and for her cutting criticism and unwavering support.
Also, for standing over my shoulder as I write this.

P.V.

For Lisa, Jack, and Sam, as always.

T.C.

CONTENTS

INTRODUCTION

You've probably seen many of the entrances in these pages, perhaps without knowing their architectural style, or the period they represent, or their place in the long, ongoing history of American home design. You may have observed that some houses draw and welcome visitors better than others, without your knowing exactly why. You may have even tried visualizing the doorways of some of them on your own home.

As you'll see, there's more to entrances than access and ingress, than doors opening and closing. Well-defined and clearly articulated entrances reveal a house's identity more readily than any other element. In some instances, they provide the only distinct clue to a home's architectural character; in others, they can blur the original style when an older structure is updated.

What's more, good entrances beckon and shelter visitors; they welcome them. They introduce the interiors—and the owners—to the street, the neighborhood, the town. Well-designed entrances also serve as a transition between the outdoors and indoors and help bring light into a house.

We're conversant with the subject. Practically all of the houses and entrances illustrated in these pages are found in the early New England town where we live, which has given us an everyday working knowledge of how these entrances function and how they might best be adapted to other houses.

We have divided *The Language of Doors* into three sections, beginning with nineteen classic entrance styles listed in chronological order and identified, illustrated, and defined. They have frequently overlapped one another and more often than not they have evolved in reaction to an older style. Their history and evolution make up the big quilt of American architecture.

The drawings in Part Two show a number of diverse classic entrances adapted to the most ubiquitous styles of American houses. These we thought are a more accessible way than a set of blueprints for readers to see and appreciate, rather than to just imagine, how these adapted entrances look.

The third part is a glossary of architectural terms and references. Knowing the names of the different entrances and of architectural details, and being able to recognize the elements that define a particular period and style, are good ways to access and understand the subject of entrances. This knowledge can also prove useful when you are talking to contractors and architects.

In the modern suburban landscape of nearly identical facades, we believe that drawing upon the past illuminates the present and enables people to reinvent their homes and their lives. It is the very sameness of so many suburban houses, in fact, that makes them such ideal candidates for transformations of this kind.

The Language of Doors isn't an exhaustive study of American architecture and entrances. It's intended as a pattern book of styles, as a handy reference for identifying architectural elements and terms, and as a guide to visualizing classic entrances on typical twentieth- and twenty-first-century American houses. Our hope is that it opens the door to a new world of possibilities for home owners everywhere.

PAULO VICENTE AND TOM CONNOR

The history of entrances is a tale of humans alternatively wanting company and wanting to be left alone.

The first doorways were openings in caves, the first doors boulders, bark and branches, and the hides of animals. Well before the dawn of Western civilization, humans were experimenting with new ways of framing openings and welcoming visitors. At Newgrange, a megalithic tomb built in Ireland five hundred years before Stonehenge, access to a one-acre burial mound is through a pair of upright stones spanned by a simple stone lintel and a roof box—a square opening serving as a primitive transom window. At daybreak during the winter solstice, sunlight enters the box and for fifteen minutes penetrates the passageway, illuminating the center of the tomb.

By the thirteenth century B.C., Greek temples such as the Lion Gate in Mycenae featured triangular stone carvings over the lintels, and by the fifth century B.C., important houses and public buildings such as the Parthenon used colonnades, or rows of columns, to connect the outdoors to the interior, and to enclose an entry porch that framed an anteroom and central doorway.

Similar in shape to cave entrances, arched entrances came to characterize and dramatize the way in. Saxon doorways, from A.D. 500 to 1066, had high, rounded arches; the most notable surviving examples are St. Peter and St. Paul churches in Canterbury. By the Romanesque period in the twelfth and thirteenth centuries, entrance arches had become broader, more rounded, and ornate. And in the succeeding Gothic period, which ranged across Europe from the twelfth to the sixteenth centuries, doors were often massive constructions of vertical boards, but entranceways had taken a distinctive and delicate turn in the form of pointed arches, such as those found at Notre-Dame in Paris.

In America, the English who settled New England brought with them building traditions from the Old World, including the Tudor-like batten door: an unframed wooden door of usually rough, vertical boards fastened to horizontal or Z-shaped battens—short horizontal strips of wood—on the inside. It wasn't just that the windowless doors were sturdy and easy to make; their main purpose was keeping uninvited callers—beasts of the forest, American Indians, and fanatical neighbors—out.

Early Colonials, Saltboxes, and Capes didn't appear much more welcoming. On Massachusetts' Cape Cod, where Capes originated in the late 1600s, unsheltered, unpainted, unornamented doorways demonstrated a kind of reverse snobbery: the more self-effacing the facade, the more proper the occupants.

By the eighteenth century, however, the door had slammed shut on Puritanism, and the front entrance became an increasingly important part of the American home. Georgians, Federals, and Greek Revivals boasted grand entrances with pediments, porticoes, columns, pilasters, sidelights, fanlights, and balconies. The Victorian era added sweeping entry porches and even more moldings and ornamentation.

All these embellishments were popular until the early twentieth century, the advent of the modern movement and, alarmingly, of the attached garage. In the sprawl of suburban development in America in the second half of the last century, the garage door at the end of the driveway usurped the front entrance as the true destination and the primary point of ingress. Some home owners were said to know of no other way into their houses.

Now, in the twenty-first century, front entrances are being rediscovered and appreciated. Seldom-used front doors are being unstuck, doorways widened, and whole facades reimagined to reclaim that entrance as the true portal into the house.

USING THIS BOOK

Since a classic entrance embodies, in a highly concentrated way, the style of the house itself, Part One represents a kind of cursory tour of 350 years of American home building. This survey helps make sense of the evolution of particular architectural periods and styles and can help form connections between past and present sensibilities.

In addition to general discussions and illustrations of the various styles of entrances, the first part describes "surrounds"—the secondary, decorative elements that typically encompass doorways—which include

- pediments, porticoes, and porches;
- columns, posts, and pilasters;
- batten, paneled, carved, and glazed doors;
- sidelights, transoms, and fanlights; and
- casings, moldings, and decorative woodwork.

If you find you are interested in adapting a classic entrance to your home, Part Two of the book, entitled Adaptations, provides what you would hire a professional to do. It imagines how a range of classic entrances—Classical Revival, Prairie, Craftsman/Bungalow, Mediterranean, Second Empire, Georgian, Federal, Italianate, Colonial Revival, Greek Revival, and Gothic Revival—would look when superimposed on four typical, ubiquitous twentieth- and twenty-first-century American houses: Ranches, Foursquares, Builders' Colonials, and Cape Cods.

You'll most likely still need to hire an architect or talented builder to draw up a set of plans, since size, proportion, and scale are essential to an entrance addition. But being able to see it in a detailed drawing will save you considerable time, money, and frustration.

The glossary at the back of the book is, of course, a dictionary of and elaboration on the architectural terms used throughout the book.

ADAPTING A CLASSIC ENTRANCE

An entrance remodel is the simplest, least expensive, and most dramatic way to transform the exterior of a house. If your house looks like a lot of the others on the street, or if the entrance to it is so nondescript that visitors take no notice of it, then you may want to consider adapting one of the classic entrances from the rendered conversions in Part Two. Choosing the right entrance has as much to do with your taste and needs as it does with the type of house you live in. Yet your choice should be informed, at least in part, by which entrance best suits the house. Some entrances and houses are natural matches.

Cape Cods' modest proportions lend themselves to Craftsman and Bungalow entrances, as well as to Colonial Revival, Greek Revival, and, surprisingly, Gothic Revival entrances. Builders' Colonials belong to the same family as Georgians and Federals, which evolved from early-Colonial-period houses. Beneath the details, the basic two-story Colonial rectangle is a suitable form for a world of other possible entrances: Italianate, Classical Revival, Victorian, Mediterranean. The plain Foursquare also easily translates into Italianate, Mediterranean, and Craftsman/Bungalow. Stretching out across the suburban landscape, Ranches share traits with Prairie and Craftsman houses, from which they partially evolved, while leaving room for conversions to everything from Classical to Art Deco and Modernist entrances. And various combinations of all of the above.

At the same time, other suburban styles seem to defy reentrancing unless they're part of a major remodeling effort that also transforms the rest of the facade. Modern-period houses, in particular—one-of-a-kinds, Contemporaries, Raised Ranches, Split Levels— are tough matches for classic entrances. With these houses, custom-designed doorways, perhaps containing a number of classical references and variations, often work best.

In general, entrances are the most successful when they

- ✍ satisfy the owners' tastes, needs, and dreams;
- ✍ suit and enhance the style of the existing house, in character if not in literal architectural style;
- ✍ are proportionate and scaled to the rest of the house;
- ✍ draw the eye to the door without overpowering the facade;
- ✍ use details and ornaments that support the entrance rather than proclaim themselves; and
- ✍ invite guests waiting for someone to answer the door to admire the details and workmanship.

Part One

CLASSIC ENTRANCES

COLONIAL PERIOD

1600 – 1830

COLONIAL STYLE
1600 – 1820

To many, "Colonial" has come to mean the kind of plain and reassuringly familiar house, frequently painted white or gray with green or black shutters, that went up in great numbers during the second half of the twentieth century and today is found in suburban developments across the country.

Although the basic shape has remained more or less the same over the centuries, present-day models are a far cry from authentic, original Colonials. Surviving examples, built roughly between the early 1600s and the early 1800s, can be found in practically any New England town. As is true of succeeding architectural styles superimposed upon American buildings, those early houses represent styles and building techniques carried over or later imported from the Old World—in particular, England.

The earliest Colonial-era houses were rectangular boxes that relied upon medieval forms and methods: timber framing, wattle and plaster walls, and thatched roofs. Architecturally, they were a mix of rustic huts, cottages, and folk dwellings. Steep roofs, massive fireplaces, and small windows recalled English Tudor buildings. But when transplanted to the New World, they differed in an important respect: The seemingly limitless forests of native oak and white pine in New England allowed colonists to construct houses that were even larger, with second stories and varied floor plans. By the end of the seventeenth century, clapboards had replaced wattle, and roofs of wood shingles had replaced thatch, which had been used in Great Britain since the Middle Ages. (Early Southern Colonials, on the other hand, were frequently built of brick, with chimneys positioned at either end of the houses rather than in the center, as in New England.)

The first New England Colonials had absolutely flat, plain facades and entrances, usually in the form of batten doors. This was partly in keeping with rural English cottage style. But the truth was that few colonists had the time or energy for anything more elaborate. Nor, in an often inhospitable land, did they necessarily want to call attention to the way in. Despite their simplicity and practicality, however, the entrances were rich in small, graceful details: diamond-headed nails arranged in patterns across the doors, hand-carved pendants suspended from second-floor overhangs, and sometimes low transom windows of two and three lights, or panes, over doors.

At the same time, settlers from other countries brought with them architectural antecedents of their own, leading to clusters of Colonials in New England and French and Spanish Colonials outside New England, each possessing its own distinct characteristics.

Long before the English settled New England, Spanish explorers laid claim to Mexico and what is now New Mexico. There, they took elements of traditional Spanish and Moorish architecture, such as open porches and stepped or curvilinear parapet walls, and mixed them with American Indian construction materials such as adobe, and features such as *vigas,* or roof beams projecting out from exterior walls. The result was a hybrid Spanish-American architecture that translated easily to Florida and California in the mid- to late seventeenth century, and to Texas in the eighteenth century.

Following a Dutch tradition in residential architecture at home, Dutch Colonials in New York and New Jersey were usually stone or brick one-and-a-half-story houses with hipped or gambrel roofs and, frequently, flared eaves. The Dutch also contributed the concept of the front stoop to the American entrance. Not surprisingly, as their presence in the New World receded, the evolution of the Dutch Colonial style slowed. (In the early 1600s, Nordic immigrants—Swedes who settled on the banks of the Delaware River—erected Scandinavian-type log houses that would become the prototype for frontier dwellings in America for the next two centuries.)

And as the French traveled south from settlements in Canada, they built houses with hipped roofs and narrow, paneled double doors, adding more variety to American dwellings. In Mississippi and Louisiana, French Colonials were distinguished by wide roof overhangs to shade one- and two-story galleries, or verandas, which often ringed the houses.

As colonists grew more prosperous, doors and doorways underwent gradual but continual change. By 1730, Colonial pragmatism had given way to fashion and style, imported from England, naturally. The basic English Colonial evolved into Georgian, then Federal, or Adam, houses with increasingly prominent entrances and doorways.

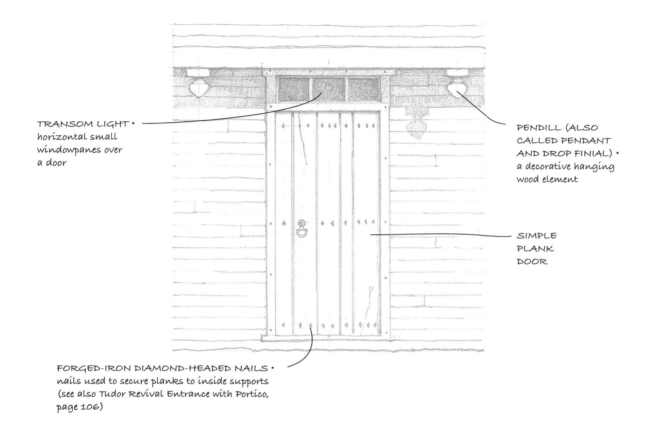

TRANSOM LIGHT •
horizontal small
windowpanes over
a door

PENDILL (ALSO
CALLED PENDANT
AND DROP FINIAL) •
a decorative hanging
wood element

SIMPLE
PLANK
DOOR

FORGED-IRON DIAMOND-HEADED NAILS •
nails used to secure planks to inside supports
(see also Tudor Revival Entrance with Portico,
page 106)

Postmedieval Colonial Entrance

By necessity, early New Englanders opted for doors that were relatively quick and easy to build. The batten, or plank, door, shown above, was the basic door on folk dwellings and postmedieval structures in England, the main country of origin for most of these settlers. The second-floor overhang, which was typical of English buildings, provided familiarity rather than, as the twentieth-century term "Garrison Colonial" implies, protection from intruders and helped stabilize the structure. It also broke up the monotony of sheer facades.

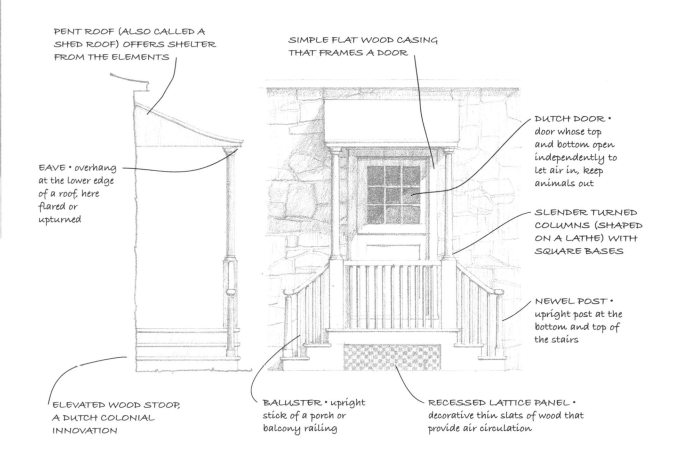

PENT ROOF (ALSO CALLED A SHED ROOF) OFFERS SHELTER FROM THE ELEMENTS

SIMPLE FLAT WOOD CASING THAT FRAMES A DOOR

DUTCH DOOR • door whose top and bottom open independently to let air in, keep animals out

EAVE • overhang at the lower edge of a roof, here flared or upturned

SLENDER TURNED COLUMNS (SHAPED ON A LATHE) WITH SQUARE BASES

NEWEL POST • upright post at the bottom and top of the stairs

ELEVATED WOOD STOOP, A DUTCH COLONIAL INNOVATION

BALUSTER • upright stick of a porch or balcony railing

RECESSED LATTICE PANEL • decorative thin slats of wood that provide air circulation

Dutch Colonial Entrance

Most of the houses built by Dutch settlers in New Amsterdam (later Manhattan) and other New World settlements were of brick or stone and featured modest wood doorways with flat, unornamented casings and a fairly simple shed roof. Although almost completely replaced by English Colonial houses, the Dutch Colonial contributed the front stoop (*stoep* in Dutch) and the Dutch door to American architecture. The ornamental lattice-work beneath the entrance kept animals from nesting under the stoop and stairs.

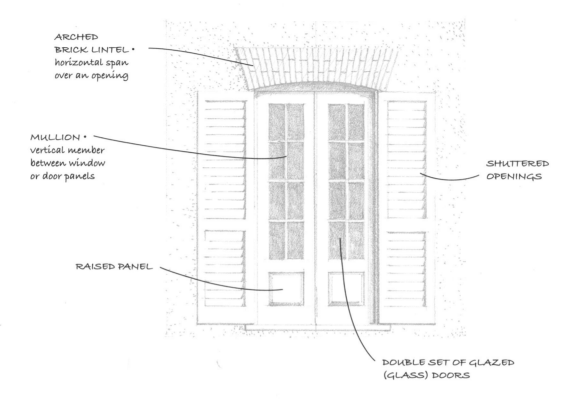

ARCHED
BRICK LINTEL •
horizontal span
over an opening

MULLION •
vertical member
between window
or door panels

SHUTTERED
OPENINGS

RAISED PANEL

DOUBLE SET OF GLAZED
(GLASS) DOORS

French Colonial Entrance

While France's presence in the New World extended from Canada to the Deep South, architecturally it was most influential in New Orleans in the nineteenth century. Tall, narrow doors, divided between lower solid panels and upper lights, or windows, were arranged in pairs—hence "French doors"—and frequently set in porches or under overhangs or balconies. Shutters (here horizontal slats, but frequently vertical planks) swung closed over the entrances for privacy and protection from the elements.

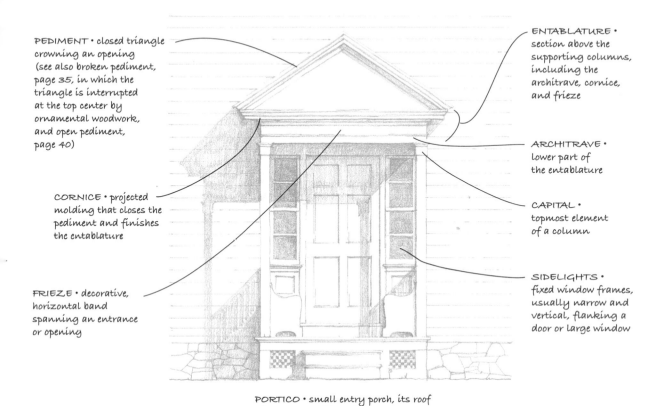

PEDIMENT • closed triangle crowning an opening (see also broken pediment, page 35, in which the triangle is interrupted at the top center by ornamental woodwork, and open pediment, page 40)

CORNICE • projected molding that closes the pediment and finishes the entablature

FRIEZE • decorative, horizontal band spanning an entrance or opening

ENTABLATURE • section above the supporting columns, including the architrave, cornice, and frieze

ARCHITRAVE • lower part of the entablature

CAPITAL • topmost element of a column

SIDELIGHTS • fixed window frames, usually narrow and vertical, flanking a door or large window

PORTICO • small entry porch, its roof often supported by columns or posts

Colonial Entrance with Portico

By the late seventeenth and early eighteenth centuries, pragmatism was losing ground to style consciousness and broader influences, such as neoclassical and Dutch, as in the recessed pediment over the door in this drawing. In moving away from postmedieval styles, houses were intent upon showing their best faces with the inclusion of paneled doors, sidelight windows, and small porch platforms.

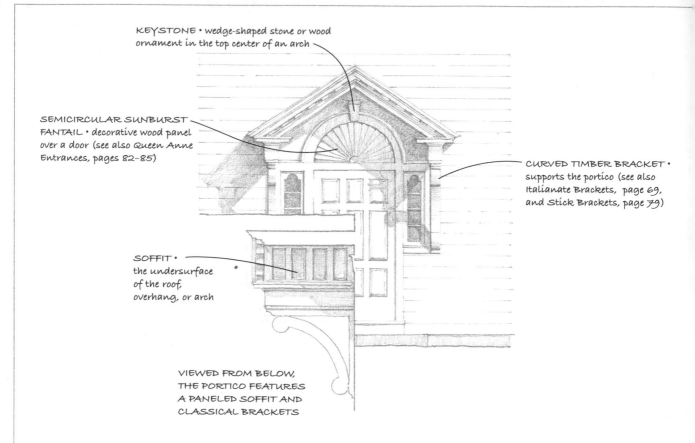

KEYSTONE • wedge-shaped stone or wood ornament in the top center of an arch

SEMICIRCULAR SUNBURST FANTAIL • decorative wood panel over a door (see also Queen Anne Entrances, pages 82–85)

CURVED TIMBER BRACKET • supports the portico (see also Italianate Brackets, page 69, and Stick Brackets, page 79)

SOFFIT • the undersurface of the roof, overhang, or arch

VIEWED FROM BELOW, THE PORTICO FEATURES A PANELED SOFFIT AND CLASSICAL BRACKETS

Late Colonial Entrance

As home owners prospered in the eighteenth century, and popular styles of the day in England reached these shores, the Colonial entrances grew more expansive, exuberant, decorative, and demonstrative. This is a transitional doorway—saying farewell to the Colonial period as it welcomes the Georgian and Federal. It is a little clunkier than either of those succeeding styles, but the influences and direction are clear: raised, nine-paneled door; Palladian-shaped sidelights; a solid fanlight in a sunburst design with ornamental keystone; and a gabled hood with rich molding and fine, curved brackets.

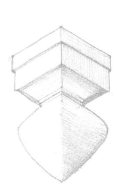

ACORN PENDANT   URN PENDANT   BALL PENDANT

Pendant Designs

An abundance of New England white pine enabled early Colonial builders and craftsmen to hand carve ornamental details such as these pendants, which typically hung from second-story overhangs. Also called pendills and drop finials, pendants were originally designed to drop from Gothic timber roofs and vaulted ceilings and later from gables, braces, and brackets. If you turn the book upside down, they appear as finials—ornaments at the top of posts, gables, and the like.

GEORGIAN STYLE
1700 – 1830

Georgian houses are characterized by the handsome symmetry of the facades around central entrances flanked by matching windows, and the formal, often ornate composition of the doorways: pilasters and sidelights on either side, a small-paned transom or intricate fanlight windows, recessed and elaborate pediments, and the liberal use of decorative woodwork and moldings.

Named after the architecture of successive reigns of English kings named George, this style, like so much of architecture, is a repository of a number of influences and elements: classical Roman, Renaissance, and that of the sixteenth-century Italian architect Andrea Palladio. These influences are recognizable in the form of pilasters, two-story porticoes, and Palladian windows. In England, the style was simultaneously referred to as Renaissance or Palladian.

In this country, the Georgian style evolved from Colonials beginning in the late seventeenth century as colonists embraced the revolutionary idea of coopting the architecture of the English ruling class. An early example was the Foster-Hutchinson House, built in Boston around 1680. Coinciding with a period of American prosperity, the style spread throughout

New England and southward, where it can be seen in mansions such as Stratford Hall and Carter's Grove, both in Virginia. By the mid-eighteenth century, it had become the preferred architecture of public buildings, churches, and colleges, such as the College of William and Mary in Williamsburg, Virginia.

America's taste for all things Georgian lasted a relatively short time — approximately from 1700 to the Revolutionary War. But from around the turn of the nineteenth century to the 1930s, a style known as Georgian Revival reclaimed some of the earlier glory of Georgian architecture in the form of mostly large, expensive houses in the Eastern suburbs and Southern cities. Many of those structures were built on a smaller scale than that of their predecessors, especially those in England. Roofs were as likely to be gambreled as gabled. Some Georgian Revival houses looked like plain Colonials dressed up in elaborate moldings, sidelights, and fanlights to resemble something grander. Fortunately, enough of the original Georgian design elements survived in the newer Georgian entrances: perfect symmetry, fine craftsmanship, and lots of detailed exterior molding.

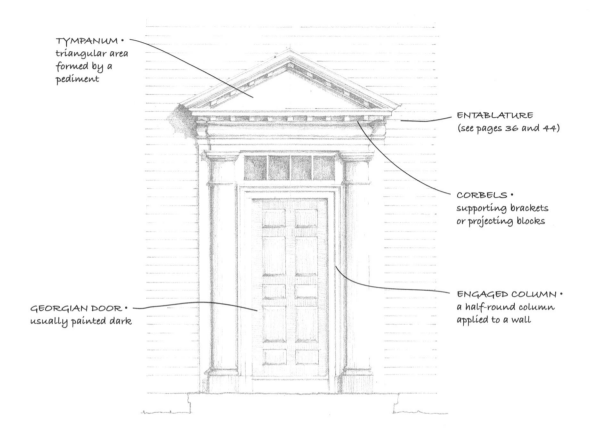

TYMPANUM •
triangular area
formed by a
pediment

ENTABLATURE
(see pages 36 and 44)

CORBELS •
supporting brackets
or projecting blocks

ENGAGED COLUMN •
a half-round column
applied to a wall

GEORGIAN DOOR •
usually painted dark

Georgian Entrance with Pediment

Georgian is an elaboration of the basic Colonial style, stating every aspect of the entrance—doors, lights, surrounds, and especially crowns (the top of a doorway)—in greater and more decorative detail. A key, emerging element was the classical pediment, which drew inspiration from the Italian Renaissance and was built in any number of forms: gabled (triangular, as shown here), segmental (curved), ogee (S-shaped), and broken (divided in half, usually with an ornament in the center).

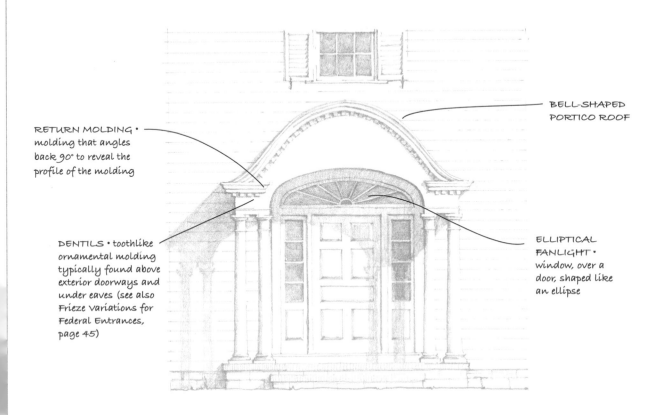

RETURN MOLDING · molding that angles back 90° to reveal the profile of the molding

BELL-SHAPED PORTICO ROOF

DENTILS · toothlike ornamental molding typically found above exterior doorways and under eaves (see also Frieze Variations for Federal Entrances, page 45)

ELLIPTICAL FANLIGHT · window, over a door, shaped like an ellipse

Georgian Entrance with Portico

The broad bell-shaped portico made possible another hallmark of Georgian entrances, the fanlight window, which is elliptical in this example. Note, too, the elaborate paneling, four-light sidelights, and flanking sets of double Tuscan columns—all intended to emphasize the grandeur of the house and the status of its owners.

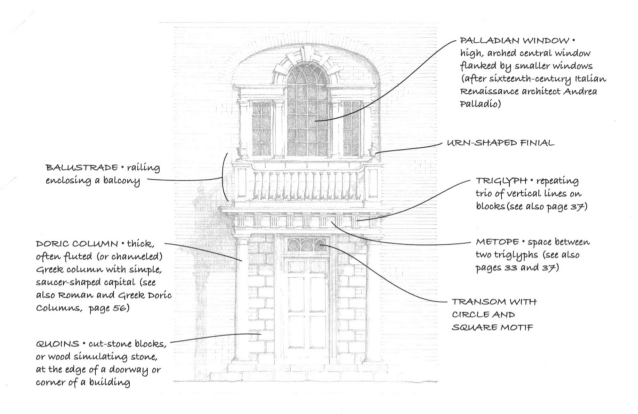

PALLADIAN WINDOW •
high, arched central window
flanked by smaller windows
(after sixteenth-century Italian
Renaissance architect Andrea
Palladio)

URN-SHAPED FINIAL

BALUSTRADE • railing
enclosing a balcony

TRIGLYPH • repeating
trio of vertical lines on
blocks (see also page 37)

DORIC COLUMN • thick,
often fluted (or channeled)
Greek column with simple,
saucer-shaped capital (see
also Roman and Greek Doric
Columns, page 56)

METOPE • space between
two triglyphs (see also
pages 33 and 37)

TRANSOM WITH
CIRCLE AND
SQUARE MOTIF

QUOINS • cut-stone blocks,
or wood simulating stone,
at the edge of a doorway or
corner of a building

Two-Story Georgian Entrance

The influence of the Italian Renaissance, which had been embraced in England more than
a century before, was fully realized in this country in two-story Georgian entrances,
sometimes set in centered, projecting gables. As shown here, they were frequently
highlighted by balconies and soaring Palladian windows. The glass bull's-eye pattern in the
transom, resembling the bottom of a bottle, is called a rondel.

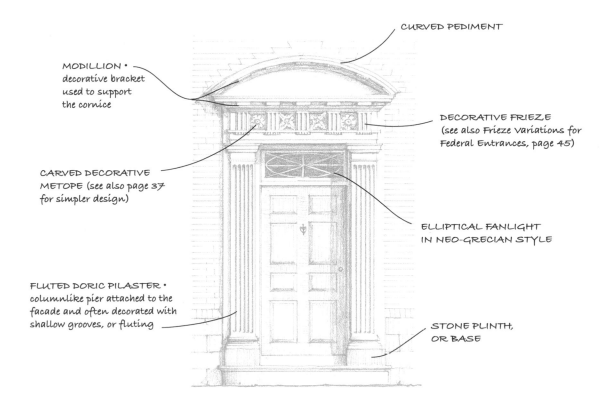

CURVED PEDIMENT

MODILLION •
decorative bracket
used to support
the cornice

DECORATIVE FRIEZE
(see also Frieze Variations for
Federal Entrances, page 45)

CARVED DECORATIVE
METOPE (see also page 37
for simpler design)

ELLIPTICAL FANLIGHT
IN NEO-GRECIAN STYLE

FLUTED DORIC PILASTER •
columnlike pier attached to the
facade and often decorated with
shallow grooves, or fluting

STONE PLINTH,
OR BASE

Georgian Entrance with Segmental Pediment

Although the segmental, or curved, pediment casts a low profile, it often crowned highly ornamented entrances, especially on elegant townhouses of brick or stone. The frieze, above the door, is representative of the kinds of sculptural designs incorporated into Georgian surrounds. Another feature of the Georgian style is the pilasters (here fluted, or decorated with shallow, vertical grooves) that flank the doorway. They maintain the doorway's relatively flat projection while calling attention to its detailing.

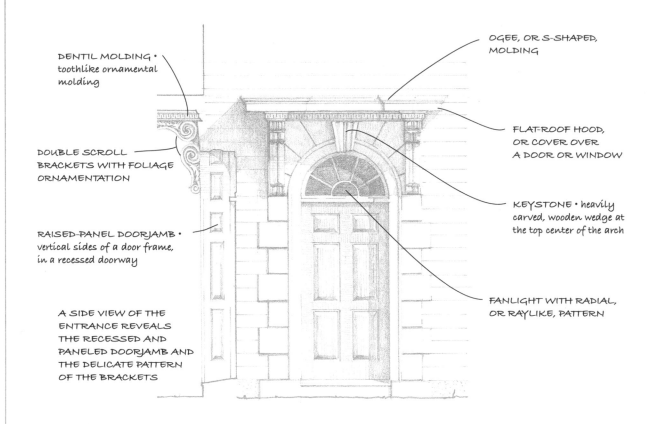

DENTIL MOLDING •
toothlike ornamental
molding

OGEE, OR S-SHAPED,
MOLDING

DOUBLE SCROLL
BRACKETS WITH FOLIAGE
ORNAMENTATION

FLAT-ROOF HOOD,
OR COVER OVER
A DOOR OR WINDOW

KEYSTONE • heavily
carved, wooden wedge at
the top center of the arch

RAISED-PANEL DOORJAMB •
vertical sides of a door frame,
in a recessed doorway

A SIDE VIEW OF THE
ENTRANCE REVEALS
THE RECESSED AND
PANELED DOORJAMB AND
THE DELICATE PATTERN
OF THE BRACKETS

FANLIGHT WITH RADIAL,
OR RAYLIKE, PATTERN

Hooded Georgian Entrance

More so than curved pediments, a flat hood is the appropriate crown to this simple but very
elegant entrance. In contrast, the brackets are highly decorative and, in an understatement,
appear to be supported by quoins rather than pilasters. Glass in the half-round fanlight is
segmented by radial muntins. The doorjambs (see the side view above left) are paneled,
mirroring the pattern in the door.

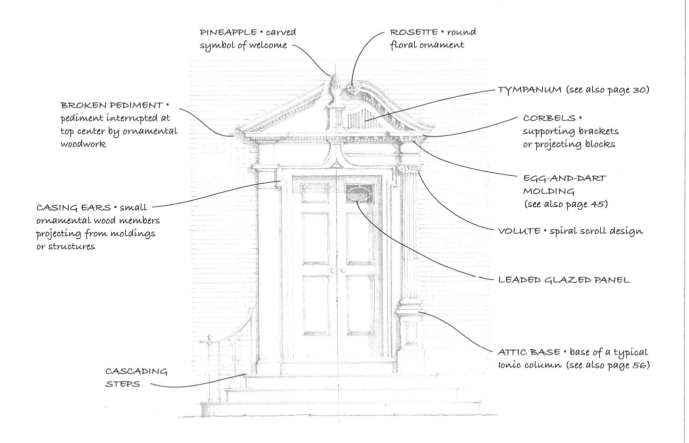

PINEAPPLE · carved symbol of welcome

ROSETTE · round floral ornament

TYMPANUM (see also page 30)

BROKEN PEDIMENT · pediment interrupted at top center by ornamental woodwork

CORBELS · supporting brackets or projecting blocks

EGG-AND-DART MOLDING (see also page 45)

CASING EARS · small ornamental wood members projecting from moldings or structures

VOLUTE · spiral scroll design

LEADED GLAZED PANEL

ATTIC BASE · base of a typical Ionic column (see also page 56)

CASCADING STEPS

Unornamented and Ornamented Georgian Entrances
with Broken Pediment

On the left side of the illustration, the gabled pediment breaks at a sharp angle and is decorated only with dental molding and a carved pineapple, often found at the entrances to great houses, whose owners entertained guests on a regular basis. On the right side, a floral rosette caps the swan-neck pediment molding. The tympanum is fluted, and the pilaster, which is flat on the other side of the double doors, is fluted and capped in the Ionic style.

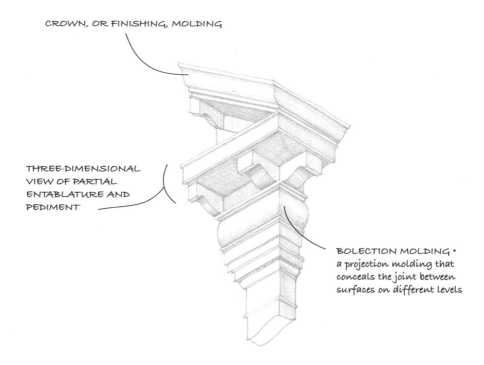

CROWN, OR FINISHING, MOLDING

THREE-DIMENSIONAL
VIEW OF PARTIAL
ENTABLATURE AND
PEDIMENT

BOLECTION MOLDING •
a projection molding that
conceals the joint between
surfaces on different levels

Georgian Cornice and Other Decorative Elements

This three-dimensional drawing of a representative Georgian pediment and surrounds, viewed from below the right corner, helps to individualize the components and put into perspective their relationship to one another, as well as the degree of thought and craftsmanship that goes into the composition.

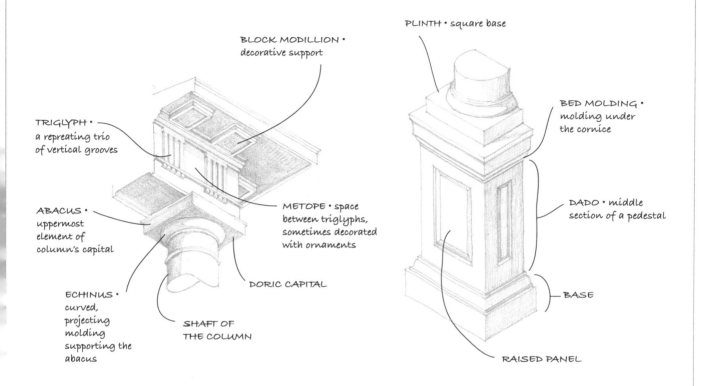

BLOCK MODILLION •
decorative support

PLINTH • square base

TRIGLYPH •
a repreating trio
of vertical grooves

BED MOLDING •
molding under
the cornice

ABACUS •
uppermost
element of
column's capital

METOPE • space
between triglyphs,
sometimes decorated
with ornaments

DADO • middle
section of a pedestal

ECHINUS •
curved,
projecting
molding
supporting the
abacus

DORIC CAPITAL

BASE

SHAFT OF
THE COLUMN

RAISED PANEL

Column, Cornice, and Pedestal Base for Georgian Columns

The column and cornice in the drawing above left are Doric, a classical Greek style characterized by simple, saucer-shaped capitals and geometric detailing. The lower section of the column in the drawing to the right sits on a rectangular pedestal that features a dado (or middle section, usually recessed) and possesses a formality that suits Georgian entrances. Many of these elements are also typically seen in Classical Revival doorways.

FEDERAL STYLE
1788 – 1820

In the wake of the American Revolution, home owners and builders shunned purely English Georgian design in favor of the noble virtues of classical Greek and Roman architecture, which seemed more in keeping with the new federation of states united under the Constitution. The origins of the Federal style, however, if not its inspiration, were British. So identified is the style with the Scottish architect Robert Adam, who mixed classical Greek and Roman elements with Renaissance and Palladian forms in designing mansions for the English upper classes, that in Europe in the mid-eighteenth century it was referred to as Adam architecture. Yet by 1788, when the first Adam-style residence was built in America, it was being called the Federal style.

Federal is more a refinement of Georgian architecture than a radical departure from it. Entrances tend to be beautifully scaled and clearly articulated; in place of sharp angles are ovals and curves. A typical doorway includes a semielliptical fanlight window over the door—or a semicircular arch housing a recessed window or decorated panel—and sidelights on either side of the door. The main distinction between Federal and Georgian entrances is a restraint in the use of decorative details. Whereas Georgian details are heavily ornate, Federals are delicate, with bas-relief ornaments of geometrical and naturalistic designs. Moldings tend to be thin and refined looking, and sidelights and transom windows shaped and leaded. Where a portico covers the doorway, the supporting pilasters will be slender and frequently tapered.

The majority of Federal houses built between the 1780s and 1820s went up along the Eastern Seaboard, where shipbuilding, whaling, and trading made sea captains wealthy and impressive homes possible. Although tall, narrow, rectangular examples exist, most of the houses were square, massive buildings, constructed both of wood and brick, which nonetheless manage to appear proportional. Their roofs are low and hipped, and frequently surrounded by balustrades.

The first house in this country to be designed in the style was The Woodlands, in Philadelphia, in 1788. The front entrance is composed of six Ionic pilasters, the rear entrance of six Doric pilasters, both under two-story porticoes. In Boston two years later, architect Charles Bulfinch designed the first of a number of Federal mansions featuring a bowed center or central projecting oval. Gore Place in Waltham, Massachusetts, is one of the best examples of a Bulfinch Federal.

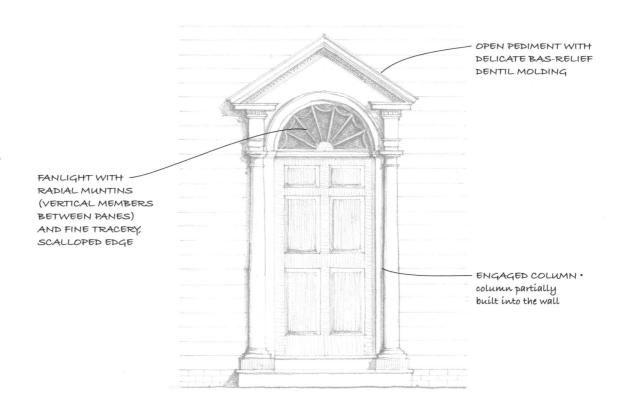

OPEN PEDIMENT WITH
DELICATE BAS-RELIEF
DENTIL MOLDING

FANLIGHT WITH
RADIAL MUNTINS
(VERTICAL MEMBERS
BETWEEN PANES)
AND FINE TRACERY,
SCALLOPED EDGE

ENGAGED COLUMN ·
column partially
built into the wall

Federal Entrance

Similar in many respects to the Georgian entrances they succeeded, Federal entrances favored curves over hard edges and delicate detailing over heavy ornamentation. Columns tended to be more slender and graceful than Georgian columns or pilasters, pediments shallower in profile, and fanlights and sometimes sidelights filled with tracery rather than square panes.

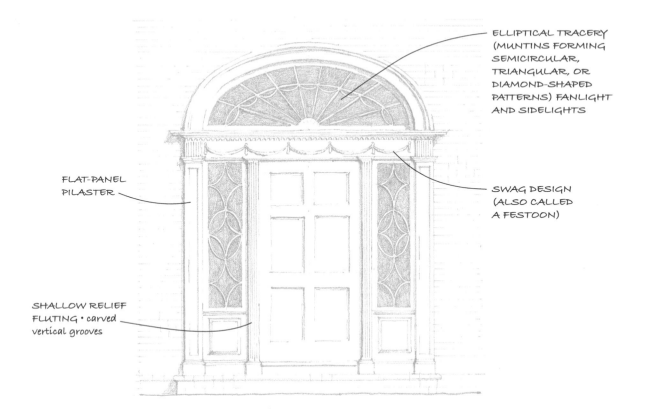

ELLIPTICAL TRACERY
(MUNTINS FORMING
SEMICIRCULAR,
TRIANGULAR, OR
DIAMOND-SHAPED
PATTERNS) FANLIGHT
AND SIDELIGHTS

FLAT-PANEL
PILASTER

SWAG DESIGN
(ALSO CALLED
A FESTOON)

SHALLOW RELIEF
FLUTING · carved
vertical grooves

Federal Entrance with Tracery Fanlight and Sidelights

Many Federal doorways were dominated by broad, elliptical fanlights, such as the one shown in this drawing. The use of leading in the transom and sidelights, as opposed to square wood mullions, permitted delicate patterns of great beauty and variety.

The frieze above this doorways displays one of the kinds of classical embellishments — in this case a thin, looping swag in bas-relief — found on Greek and Roman monuments, which inspired the style in England.

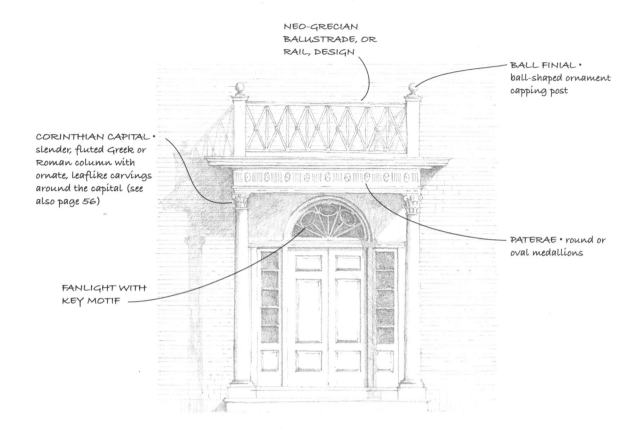

NEO-GRECIAN BALUSTRADE, OR RAIL, DESIGN

BALL FINIAL • ball-shaped ornament capping post

CORINTHIAN CAPITAL • slender, fluted Greek or Roman column with ornate, leaflike carvings around the capital (see also page 56)

PATERAE • round or oval medallions

FANLIGHT WITH KEY MOTIF

Federal Entrance with Balcony

Compared with balconies over Georgian doorways, especially those dominated by Palladian windows, Federal balconies appear modest. So does the handsome frieze of alternating fluting and paterae, a decorative round or oval medallion (see also Frieze Variations for Federal Entrances, page 45). Yet they signaled the home owner's wealth and gentility every bit as assuredly, if not as loudly. The columns framing the entrance are Corinthian. The balustrade is neoclassical, as is the semicircular transom with spokes and key motif.

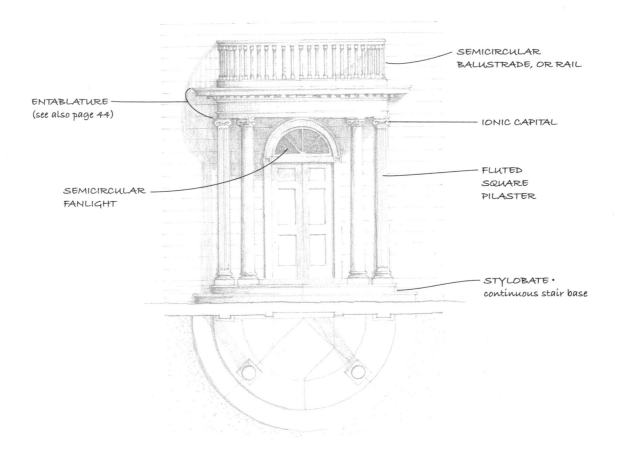

ENTABLATURE
(see also page 44)

SEMICIRCULAR
BALUSTRADE, OR RAIL

IONIC CAPITAL

SEMICIRCULAR
FANLIGHT

FLUTED
SQUARE
PILASTER

STYLOBATE ·
continuous stair base

Federal Entrance with Rounded Balcony

"Simple elegance" might have been accurately applied for the first time in America to Federal entrances such as this one. The scale of the elements and disparate forms—curves, uprights, flat and rounded surfaces—is sublime. Spaced columns (here, twin sets of Corinthian columns and pilasters) were a trademark of Robert Adam. The rounded front stoop mirrors the balcony and serves as a solid platform for the entire composition.

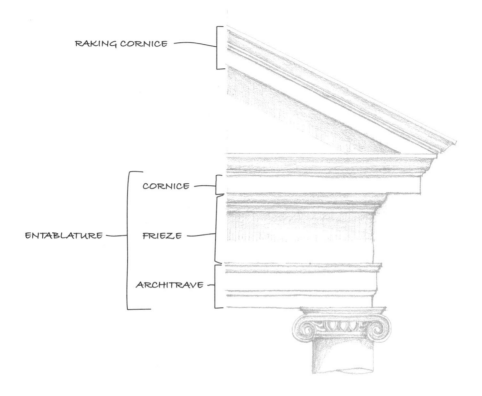

RAKING CORNICE

CORNICE

ENTABLATURE

FRIEZE

ARCHITRAVE

Entablature

The entablature is the section of a doorway casing between the capital (or top of a column) and the roof or edge of a pediment or portico. In classical architecture (and therefore, typically, on Georgian, Federalist, and Greek Revival doorways), it is made up of three parts: architrave, which is the lower molding resting on the capital; frieze, the decorative horizontal band spanning the doorway; and cornice, the upper projecting molding that finishes a pediment or portico.

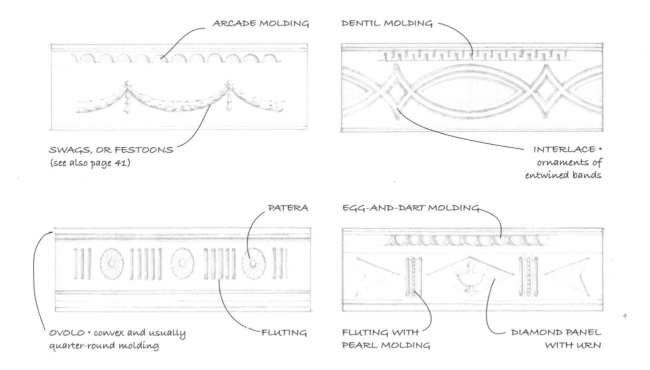

ARCADE MOLDING

DENTIL MOLDING

SWAGS, OR FESTOONS
(see also page 41)

INTERLACE •
ornaments of
entwined bands

PATERA

EGG-AND-DART MOLDING

OVOLO • convex and usually
quarter-round molding

FLUTING

FLUTING WITH
PEARL MOLDING

DIAMOND PANEL
WITH URN

Frieze Variations for Federal Entrances

On classical buildings, a frieze, the horizontal plate resting on columns and spanning entrances, was usually adorned with relief sculptures of the gods or decorative designs. The rich variety of ornamental details found in Federal friezes is largely the legacy of British architect Robert Adam, who was influenced by early Greek and Roman monuments and who, in turn, influenced the Federal period in late-eighteenth-century America. Frieze patterns typically include bas-relief urns, paterae, sheaths of wheat, festoons (also called swags), triglyphs, diamonds, and borders of decorative moldings.

CLASSICAL REVIVAL STYLE
1770 – 1830

From the time before the American Revolution, and especially after the War of 1812, American architects freely borrowed forms and details from the architecture of ancient Greece and Rome in order to embody the ideals of liberty, democracy, and a sense of civic duty in the buildings they designed.

Although since the late 1600s Colonial houses had been ennobled by the addition of classical, columned porticoes, the Classical Revival style became the widely accepted architecture of the New Republic. It naturally suited national monuments and institutions—the United States Capitol in Washington, D.C., is designed in the style—and also private residences, which were built from builders' guides published in the early nineteenth century.

Classical Revival entrances are characterized by colonnades of ordered columns, often Roman Doric or Tuscan, which supported impressive porticoes, and recessed and often ornamented gables that were capped (at least on public buildings and the grandest mansions) with domes. The prominent entrance feature, however, is a portico with a central gable and, frequently, Federal-style fanlight windows and trim. Southern Classical Revival mansions typically feature monumental two-story porticoes with four to eight columns.

As such, Classical Revival bridged the Colonial and Romantic periods, setting the stage for Greek and Gothic Revivals and Italianate houses that stirred the imaginations of the American public for the next half century.

Another influence on the style was Thomas Jefferson, considered the father of American public buildings and monumental homes. Jefferson possessed a strong, personal sense of design, as well as a bedrock belief that his tastes represented the country's. Many of the finest examples of Classical Revival buildings came about as a result of either his involvement or his insistence: the Virginia state capitol, numerous buildings at the University of Virginia, and Monticello, his house. Designed by him as a monument to himself and to the country, Monticello was inspired by the four years Jefferson spent in Paris as United States ambassador to France, as well as by Palladio. The main sections of the mansion are linked to its wings in the style of ancient Roman villas.

So resoundingly were the Georgian and Federal styles abandoned in paying homage to Rome that, just before its completion as a Georgian manor, Jefferson began remodeling Monticello in the classical Roman style. By the time the house was completed in 1830, Classical Revivalism had been eclipsed, in turn, by the Greek Revival style.

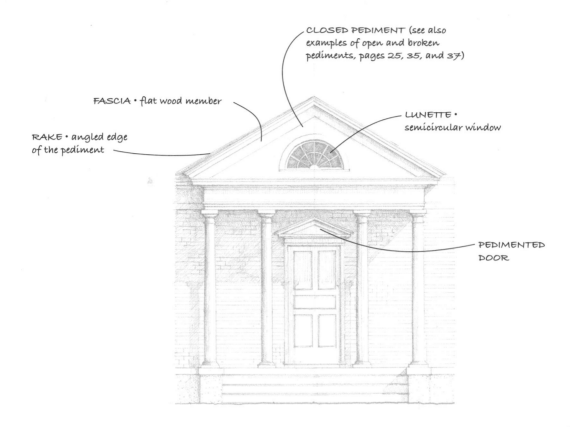

CLOSED PEDIMENT (see also examples of open and broken pediments, pages 25, 35, and 37)

FASCIA • flat wood member

RAKE • angled edge of the pediment

LUNETTE • semicircular window

PEDIMENTED DOOR

Classical Revival Entrance

Classical Revival represents the last stage of Colonial evolution and the beginning of the Romantic period of revival houses. Signature full-story entrance porticoes, made more prominent by gables that towered above Federal doorways, elevated the houses to monuments. Though spare in ornamentation, Classical Revival entrances were nonetheless grand, using scale to create presence.

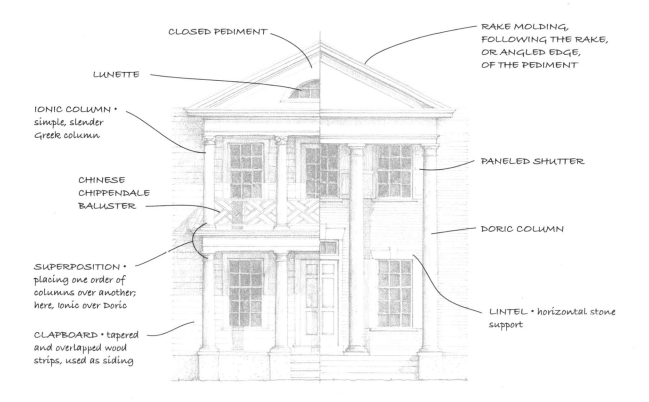

CLOSED PEDIMENT

LUNETTE

IONIC COLUMN •
simple, slender
Greek column

CHINESE
CHIPPENDALE
BALUSTER

SUPERPOSITION •
placing one order of
columns over another;
here, Ionic over Doric

CLAPBOARD • tapered
and overlapped wood
strips, used as siding

RAKE MOLDING,
FOLLOWING THE RAKE,
OR ANGLED EDGE,
OF THE PEDIMENT

PANELED SHUTTER

DORIC COLUMN

LINTEL • horizontal stone
support

Classical Revival Entrance
with Full-Story and Two-Tiered Porticoes

On the right, above, is a full two-story portico supported by Doric columns. Flared lintels
with keystones over the windows and doors are a detail imported from France, whose own
fight for independence resonated in the United States. On the left, a more elaborate two-
tiered portico of the kind favored in Southern Classical Revival houses, has a broad
lunette in the gable eave. The lower columns are Doric; for variation, the upper are Ionic.
The baluster design is Chinese Chippendale.

ROMANTIC PERIOD

1820 – 1890

GREEK REVIVAL STYLE
1818 – 1880

Architectural styles frequently develop in reaction to preceding styles and in response to changing ideas and tastes. This was especially true in a country on a fast track to discover itself and to create a history and culture of its own, as America was in the nineteenth century. As Thomas Jefferson had embraced Roman ideals, so the next generation embraced Greek architecture.

Greek Revival houses and entrances might easily be included with Classical Revival, since both drew on similar references: the principles of Greek democracy as expressed in classical design. As such, it was the perfect style for expressing the values of a young America. The style also naturally fit into the romantic view of houses that flourished in this country at the time, which favored the symbolic and sentimental over the rational.

More prominent and widespread than buildings designed in the Roman style of the Classical Revival period were Greek Revival buildings, which began appearing around 1820. For the most part, the style adapted classical masonry forms to American wood construction techniques, producing a remarkable number of magnificent mansions—the trophy houses of the day—that were usually painted white, as if to simulate temple marble. These are found not only on the New England coast, where Yankee sea captains perhaps identified with the ancient seafarers of the Greek isles, but elsewhere in the Northeast and also in the South: the Bowers House in Northampton, Massachusetts, for example, and the Lee Mansion in Arlington, Virginia. Late in the heyday of the style, Greek Revival buildings of granite and marble became the ideal form for government, commercial, and public edifices across the country: the U.S. Treasury Department building in Washington, D.C.; the Second Bank of the United States in Philadelphia (built in 1818 and now called the Customs House); and capitol buildings in many states.

Greek Revival entrances had a sculptural presence that signified the permanence of the American experiment and elevated house building to a noble art. At the same time, they honored those very American ideals of ambition and success and, naturally, their owners' accomplishments.

These entrances tend to feature either prominent, projecting porticoes or broad pediments with low-pitched roofs and often a tympanum. In some Greek Revivals, the portico runs the width of the house, and the roof ridge extends from front to back. In other, usually smaller houses, the exteriors are stripped of ornamentation, and the door-ways are spanned by a simple lintel rather than an arch.

Greek Revival entrances are also characterized by thick, unadorned moldings, solid transoms (as opposed to transom or fanlight windows typically found in Classical Revival doorways), and columns conforming to the classical Greek order: heavy, simple columns with rounded capitals; slender, fluted Corinthian columns decorated with acanthus leaf detail; or Ionic columns whose capitals are decorated with double spirals.

In effect, Greek Revival buildings were domestic temples in which Americans could feel at home. By the mid-nineteenth century, Greek Revival had become widely accepted as a national style for houses.

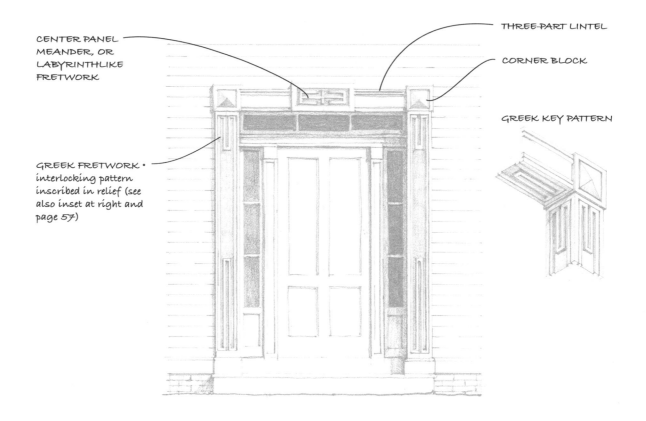

CENTER PANEL MEANDER, OR LABYRINTHLIKE FRETWORK

THREE-PART LINTEL

CORNER BLOCK

GREEK KEY PATTERN

GREEK FRETWORK · interlocking pattern inscribed in relief (see also inset at right and page 57)

Greek Revival Entrance

The clean asceticism of classical Greek temples fit nicely with the native sensibility in New England, where the first Greek Revival houses were built along the coast. Fortunes made during the first half of the nineteenth century inevitably created bloated, full-frontal caricatures of the style, but bold, simple examples, such as this, also abounded. The all-but-flat doorway enframement is graced by fretwork on the pilasters and frieze and by typically narrow transom and sidelights.

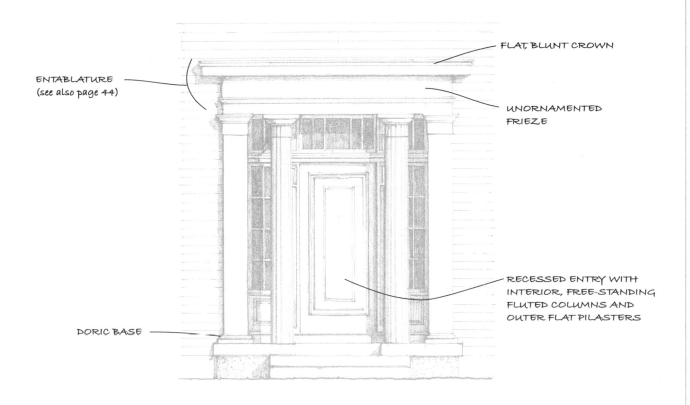

ENTABLATURE
(see also page 44)

FLAT, BLUNT CROWN

UNORNAMENTED
FRIEZE

RECESSED ENTRY WITH
INTERIOR, FREE-STANDING
FLUTED COLUMNS AND
OUTER FLAT PILASTERS

DORIC BASE

Greek Revival Entrance with Hood

Recessed doorways, framed in many instances by simple cornices, provided cool respite
from the street and the world and served as a kind of exterior foyer or anteroom. The
single-panel door is further screened by Doric columns without bases. Plain pilasters flank
and help encase the surround.

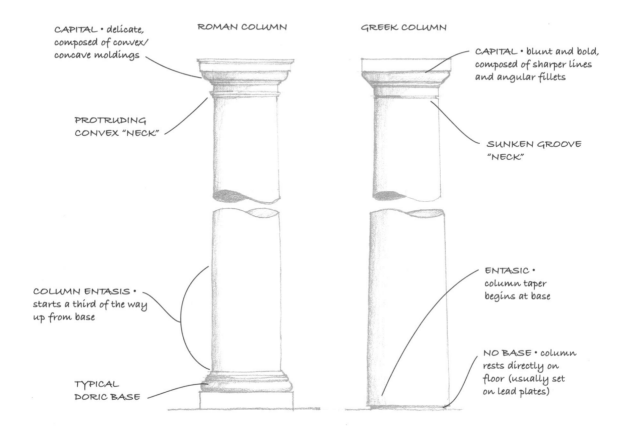

CAPITAL • delicate, composed of convex/concave moldings

ROMAN COLUMN

GREEK COLUMN

CAPITAL • blunt and bold, composed of sharper lines and angular fillets

PROTRUDING CONVEX "NECK"

SUNKEN GROOVE "NECK"

COLUMN ENTASIS • starts a third of the way up from base

ENTASIC • column taper begins at base

TYPICAL DORIC BASE

NO BASE • column rests directly on floor (usually set on lead plates)

Roman and Greek Doric Columns

Both classical Roman and Greek columns in the Doric style share a number of characteristics: round columns (as opposed to square posts) and plain capitals (as opposed to the more elaborate and ornate capitals found on Corinthian and Ionic columns). They vary, however, in several respects. Roman columns usually rest on plain pedestals and simple bases and feature a protruding ornamental band below the capital. Greek columns rest directly on the floor and have a sunken band below the capital.

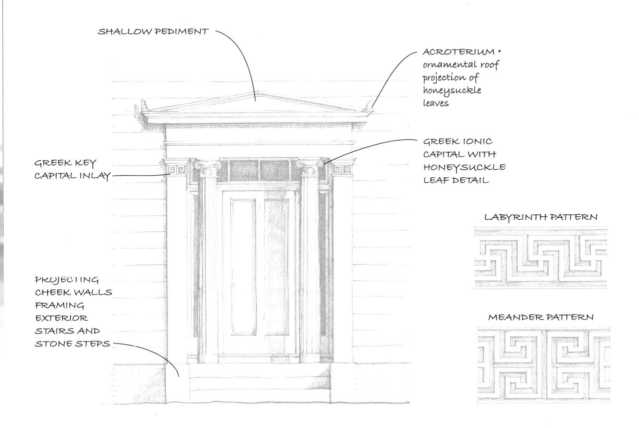

SHALLOW PEDIMENT

ACROTERIUM •
ornamental roof
projection of
honeysuckle
leaves

GREEK KEY
CAPITAL INLAY

GREEK IONIC
CAPITAL WITH
HONEYSUCKLE
LEAF DETAIL

PROJECTING
CHEEK WALLS
FRAMING
EXTERIOR
STAIRS AND
STONE STEPS

LABYRINTH PATTERN

MEANDER PATTERN

Greek Revival Entrance with Pediment

Another hallmark of the style was a low, wide, shallow pediment capping a plain frieze, architrave, and pilasters. On the flat, unembellished surround, what details there are stand out: a Greek key design at the top of the pilasters, volutes on the column capitals, and acroteria at the corners of the pediment. The stone cheek walls bookending the steps double as bases for the pilasters. Decorative borders, such as the ones above right, are called key patterns—designs of interlocking and repeated lines—and were frequently painted, inscribed, or formed on these entrances.

GOTHIC REVIVAL STYLE
1830 – 1900

Perhaps it was nostalgia for the Colonial past that inspired American architects just before and after the Civil War to romanticize Great Britain's Middle Ages in embracing the Gothic Revival style.

Gothic had been the ruling architecture in Western Europe for nearly four centuries, at least for castles, cathedrals, and academic campus buildings. It was characterized by vaults, flying buttresses, gargoyles, pinnacles, and battlements. In England, where it developed in the middle of the eighteenth century, Gothic Revival was considered "picturesque," meaning both quaint and natural. Gothic Revival houses in this country were cozier than both true English Gothic and Classical Revival structures, designed for the country rather than the city, and constructed of wood more often than stone.

Gothic Revival became the rage in America after house plans appeared in Alexander Jackson Davis's 1837 *Rural Residences* and, later, in the works of the mid-nineteenth-century landscape architect Andrew Jackson Downing, particularly his *Cottage Residences* and *The Architecture of Country Houses*. Also influential were the essays of John Ruskin, who advocated eclectic mixes of materials, colors, and other architectural styles, and two popular novelists: Sir Walter Scott, whose romantic tales of the Middle Ages and descriptions of Gothic buildings in novels such as *Ivanhoe* and *Rob Roy* made the style come alive for the general public; and James Fenimore Cooper, who remodeled his Federalist family homestead in Cooperstown, New York, in the Gothic Revival style and called it Ostego Hall.

American Carpenter Gothic–style houses of the 1830s and 1840s were stone designs interpreted in wood. From the mid- to late nineteenth century, Gothic Revival cottages popped up on the landscape from Maine to California. What characterizes the houses is multiple gables, including an off center entry gable, partial or full-width porches, and sometimes a tower. Doorways are wide and set under broad, pointed Gothic arches — the arch being the architectural feature most closely associated with the old Gothic style. In medieval churches, it represented an advancement in construction techniques over the Romanesque arch and also the spiritual aspirations of the faithful. In Gothic Revival, however, the pointed arch served as a romantic evocation of the past. The other defining features of the style are the steep-pitched gable roofs rising above the entrance and the wide trim boards (called vergeboards or bargeboards) running up the edges of the gables, which usually are decorated with lacy, decorative cutouts or scrollwork.

In addition to Carpenter Gothic, Gothic Revival evolved into several variations, including High Victorian Gothic and Collegiate Gothic, illustrated by campus buildings across the country, for example, those at Princeton and Yale, Bryn Mawr and the University of Pennsylvania, Kenyon College, Duke, and the University of Chicago.

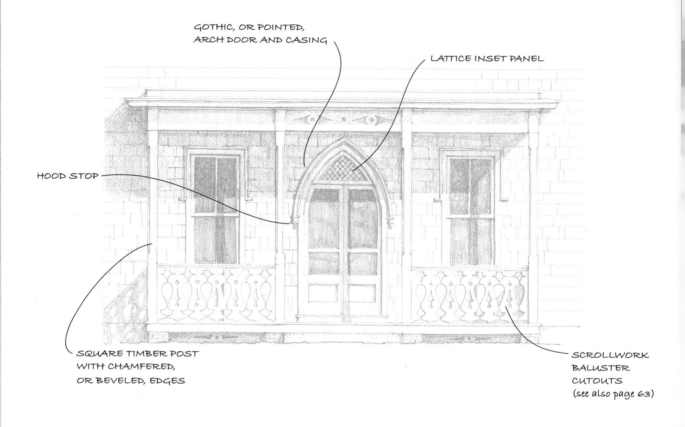

GOTHIC, OR POINTED, ARCH DOOR AND CASING

LATTICE INSET PANEL

HOOD STOP

SQUARE TIMBER POST WITH CHAMFERED, OR BEVELED, EDGES

SCROLLWORK BALUSTER CUTOUTS (see also page 63)

Gothic Revival Entrance

Perhaps the only architectural connections between Gothic cathedrals and castles of the High Middle Ages and Gothic Revival houses from the mid-1800s were the Gothic arched window, doorway, and surrounding molding, which was shaped to resemble stone. Far closer in style and scale to those of woodland cottages than those of cathedrals or castles, most Gothic Revival entrances were set inside one-story, full- or three-quarter-length porches and behind scroll saw–cut balustrades.

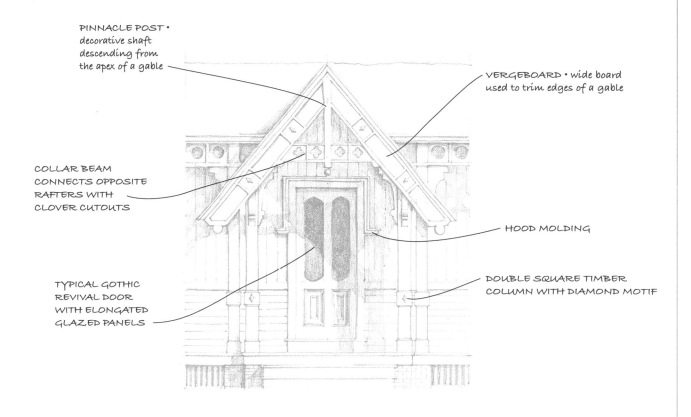

PINNACLE POST • decorative shaft descending from the apex of a gable

VERGEBOARD • wide board used to trim edges of a gable

COLLAR BEAM CONNECTS OPPOSITE RAFTERS WITH CLOVER CUTOUTS

HOOD MOLDING

TYPICAL GOTHIC REVIVAL DOOR WITH ELONGATED GLAZED PANELS

DOUBLE SQUARE TIMBER COLUMN WITH DIAMOND MOTIF

Gothic Revival Entrance with Portico

A variation on the front entry porch was the steeply gabled portico, usually trimmed with decorative vergeboards, collar beams, and pinnacle posts, and supported by shaped posts and decorative brackets. Cutouts in the trim boards leavened the severity of the steep roofs and arches, giving Gothic Revival houses a fanciful appeal.

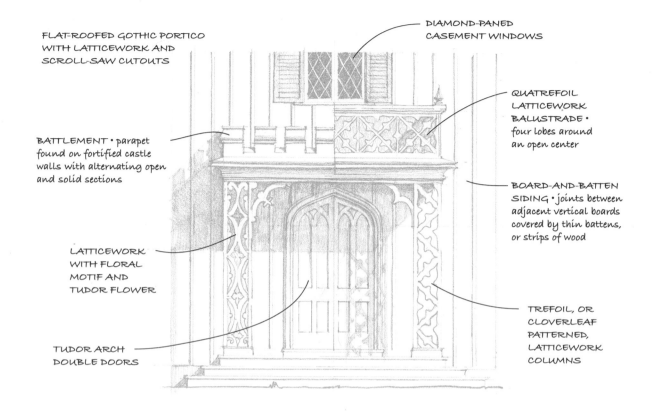

FLAT-ROOFED GOTHIC PORTICO
WITH LATTICEWORK AND
SCROLL-SAW CUTOUTS

DIAMOND-PANED
CASEMENT WINDOWS

QUATREFOIL
LATTICEWORK
BALUSTRADE •
four lobes around
an open center

BATTLEMENT • parapet
found on fortified castle
walls with alternating open
and solid sections

BOARD-AND-BATTEN
SIDING • joints between
adjacent vertical boards
covered by thin battens,
or strips of wood

LATTICEWORK
WITH FLORAL
MOTIF AND
TUDOR FLOWER

TREFOIL, OR
CLOVERLEAF
PATTERNED,
LATTICEWORK
COLUMNS

TUDOR ARCH
DOUBLE DOORS

Gothic Revival Entrance with Balcony

Gothic Revival doors were often double and elaborately paneled and frequently repeated
the Gothic arch motif. Scrollwork (or lacework)—intricate designs in columns, trim boards,
and balustrades—decorates the second-story balcony in the above drawing on the right.
On the left, crenellated molding below the window recalls, in an abstract and distant way,
the battlements of castles. In contrast, the board-and-batten siding is a casual, rural look.

Gothic Revival Scrollwork Variations

The invention of the scroll saw allowed carpenters to cut intricate patterns into single solid pieces of wood, approximating on a smaller and more modest scale tracery found in the great medieval cathedrals of Europe.

ITALIANATE STYLE
1832 – 1885

In the New World's fascination with the Old World, few houses appeared more romantic to Americans in the mid- to late nineteenth century than Italian farmhouses and Tuscan villas — the models for the Italianate style that flourished during that period. Once again, an architectural style gained national popularity in reaction to the formalism and restraint of earlier styles. In the 1880s, Italianate houses stretched from the northeastern coast, across the Midwest, to the West Coast and, in particular, San Francisco.

Although basically two-story square or rectangular boxes with asymmetrical facades, the houses also have an informality and a stateliness that make them appear both welcoming and grand, as well as practical and picturesque: In their day Italianate houses were thought to be slightly eccentric looking.

Italianate houses are identifiable by a number of features, including low-pitched hipped roofs, colonnaded porches or verandas with balconies, overhanging eaves adorned with rows of brackets (there for visual support rather than structural support), and sometimes a square or octagonal tower or a cupola on the roof.

Perhaps the most distinctive feature of Italianate entrances is the rounded arch positioned over doorways as well as windows and often capped with a decorative keystone in the center. Since the entranceways are broad and gently U-shaped, they usually have double doors fitted with large panes of glass, again matching the window crowns and the scale of the house.

One of the best-known Italianate mansions open to the public is Sunnyside, the Tarrytown, New York, estate of Washington Irving, author of "The Legend of Sleepy Hollow." The Italianate style was also used for urban row houses from the 1840s on, most notably in the form of brownstones in Manhattan and Brooklyn, New York, and for wooden houses in San Francisco.

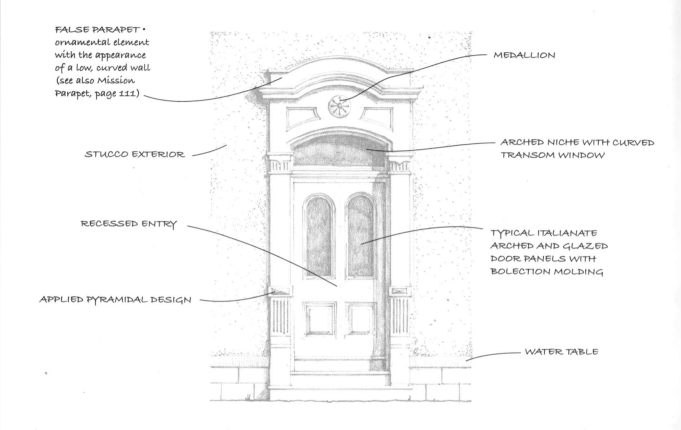

FALSE PARAPET • ornamental element with the appearance of a low, curved wall (see also Mission Parapet, page 111)

MEDALLION

STUCCO EXTERIOR

ARCHED NICHE WITH CURVED TRANSOM WINDOW

RECESSED ENTRY

TYPICAL ITALIANATE ARCHED AND GLAZED DOOR PANELS WITH BOLECTION MOLDING

APPLIED PYRAMIDAL DESIGN

WATER TABLE

Italianate Entrance

Where Federal and Greek Revival entrance architecture tend to be restrained, Italianate entrances are large, operatic, even voluptuous in their forms and rich use of ornate brackets. Arches and curves define the spirit of the style: The arched and inverted U-shape designs found in Italianate window crowns also appeared in glazed doors, sidelights, transoms, and pediments or hoods, such as this one, capped with a false parapet.

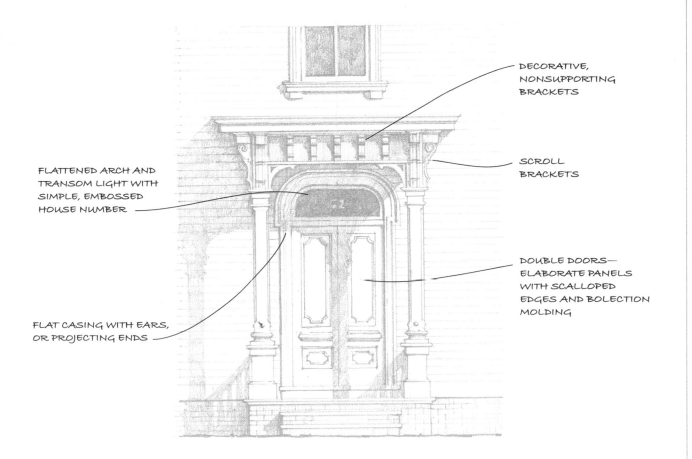

DECORATIVE, NONSUPPORTING BRACKETS

SCROLL BRACKETS

FLATTENED ARCH AND TRANSOM LIGHT WITH SIMPLE, EMBOSSED HOUSE NUMBER

DOUBLE DOORS— ELABORATE PANELS WITH SCALLOPED EDGES AND BOLECTION MOLDING

FLAT CASING WITH EARS, OR PROJECTING ENDS

Italianate Entrance with Flat-Roofed Portico

The flattened arch of the transom and casing in this drawing and the lack of division in the transom glazing give the double doors a solidity and presence that are strongly appealing. House numbers frequently appear in these open expanses of glass. The transom casing also crowns the doorway by virtue of the ears that extend beyond the vertical lengths of molding.

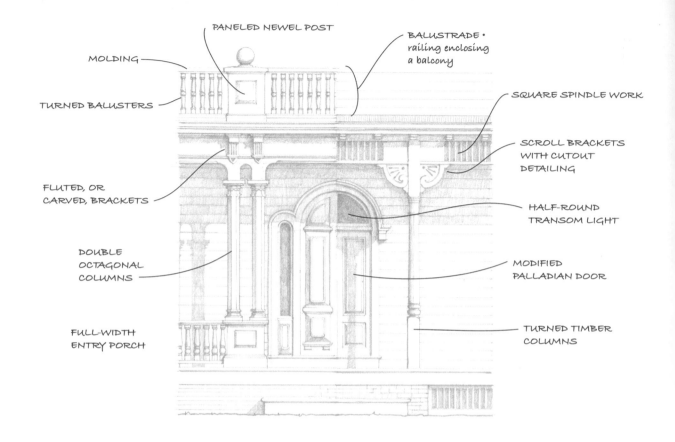

MOLDING

PANELED NEWEL POST

BALUSTRADE ·
railing enclosing
a balcony

TURNED BALUSTERS

SQUARE SPINDLE WORK

SCROLL BRACKETS
WITH CUTOUT
DETAILING

FLUTED, OR
CARVED, BRACKETS

HALF-ROUND
TRANSOM LIGHT

DOUBLE
OCTAGONAL
COLUMNS

MODIFIED
PALLADIAN DOOR

FULL-WIDTH
ENTRY PORCH

TURNED TIMBER
COLUMNS

Italianate Entry Porch

Entry porches, frequently running the width of the house, reiterated the informal,
rambling nature of rural Italian farmhouses, upon which the Italianate style was modeled
(at least at the outset). But the abundance of moldings, panels, brackets, and other
decorative details offset suggestions of rustication. Above, on the right, a turned porch
post ends in brackets of fine scrollwork. On the left, the narrow sidelight repeats the arch
of the transom and doorway between classical balustrades and thick paneled base. The
newel post on the balcony is capped with a ball finial.

SCROLL BRACKET WITH
BLOCK MODILLION

COVED, OR CONCAVE, BRACKET
WITH REGLETS—FLAT, NARROW
PROJECTIONS BETWEEN
GROOVES—AND INSET FLORAL
DECORATION

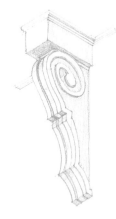 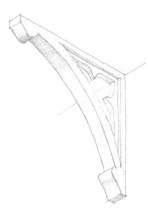  

OGEE TIP BRACKET WITH
INSET TREFOIL, OR
CLOVERLEAF, PANEL

UNENGAGED BRACKET,
ATTACHED ONLY PARTIALLY
TO THE WALL AND
OVERHANG, WITH SCROLL
MOTIF AND DROP ORNAMENT

Italianate Brackets

Italianate architecture raised the bracket to an art. Since most brackets tend to be more decorative than structural, and since these needed to be both oversize to complement the wide eaves and designed in the style of the house, Italianate brackets are visually impressive and voluptuous.

VICTORIAN PERIOD

1855 – 1910

SECOND EMPIRE STYLE
1855 – 1908

Remember Norman Bates's house high on the hill behind the motel in Alfred Hitchcock's *Psycho*? That creepy edifice with its eyelike dormers and iron crestings was Second Empire in style. In the latter half of the nineteenth century, when buildings like this began appearing in the United States, they were considered progressive and fashionable.

Second Empire refers to the architecture during the reign of Napoleon III (not to be confused with Napoleon Bonaparte's First Empire) in France in the middle of the nineteenth century, when Paris was transformed into a city of broad boulevards lined with tall, narrow, elegant buildings. Unlike the revival movements that had dictated so much of the architecture on both continents, Second Empire drew inspiration from contemporary Paris fashion and style. The buildings were more elaborate and "European" than Italianate buildings, and more vertical.

The most distinctive feature of the style is the mansard roof. Named after architect François Mansart, it is composed of nearly vertical, double slopes that make attic floors habitable. Rounded, arched, or barrel-vaulted dormers are often set into the upper walls and roofs, and decorative curbs at roof edges.

Here, however, Second Empire houses were Americanized by the addition of large verandas and diagonal or vertical exterior cladding and ornamentation. Popular in the 1860s and 1870s, they were also broader and more rambling than the French models and more eclectic, composed of a variety of sources and influences. Like those of Italianate houses, which they closely resemble, Second Empire entrances are often double doored and arched, beneath single-story porches with classical pediments, paired columns or pilasters, and they sometimes feature a balustrade above the porch.

Second Empire was the chosen style for a number of prominent mansions and civic and academic campus buildings in the latter half of the nineteenth century and first decade of the twentieth century. These include the James O. Inman house in Burrillville, Rhode Island; the Providence, Rhode Island, city hall; Main Hall at Vassar College; and the Singer Building, built in 1908, in New York City.

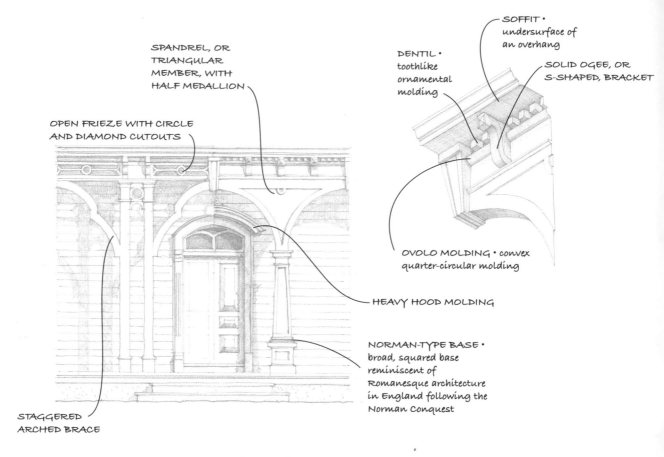

SOFFIT • undersurface of an overhang

DENTIL • toothlike ornamental molding

SOLID OGEE, OR S-SHAPED, BRACKET

SPANDREL, OR TRIANGULAR MEMBER, WITH HALF MEDALLION

OPEN FRIEZE WITH CIRCLE AND DIAMOND CUTOUTS

OVOLO MOLDING • convex quarter-circular molding

HEAVY HOOD MOLDING

NORMAN-TYPE BASE • broad, squared base reminiscent of Romanesque architecture in England following the Norman Conquest

STAGGERED ARCHED BRACE

Second Empire Entrance

Closely related to Italianate, Second Empire houses are mainly distinguished by the style's most common roof form, mansard. Second Empire entrances feature slightly more varied and eclectic details: flared gable pediments, divided transoms, and keystones and other ornaments. In the larger illustration, on the right, for example, the ornate post on a pedestal is tapered and paneled. On the left, staggered arched braces flare off slender porch posts. The open frieze showcases circle and diamond cutouts.

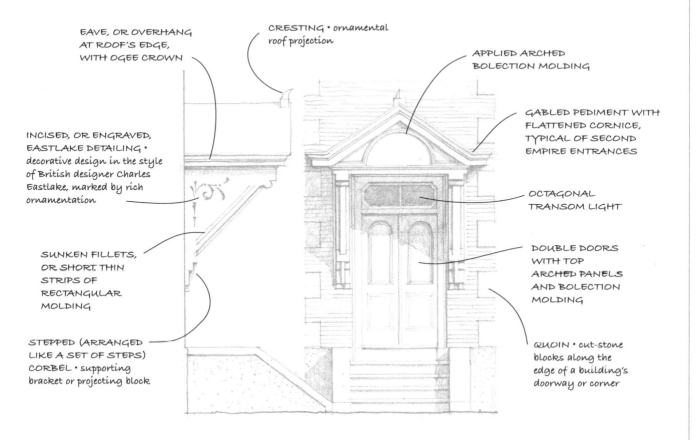

EAVE, OR OVERHANG AT ROOF'S EDGE, WITH OGEE CROWN

CRESTING · ornamental roof projection

APPLIED ARCHED BOLECTION MOLDING

GABLED PEDIMENT WITH FLATTENED CORNICE, TYPICAL OF SECOND EMPIRE ENTRANCES

INCISED, OR ENGRAVED, EASTLAKE DETAILING · decorative design in the style of British designer Charles Eastlake, marked by rich ornamentation

OCTAGONAL TRANSOM LIGHT

SUNKEN FILLETS, OR SHORT, THIN STRIPS OF RECTANGULAR MOLDING

DOUBLE DOORS WITH TOP ARCHED PANELS AND BOLECTION MOLDING

STEPPED (ARRANGED LIKE A SET OF STEPS) CORBEL · supporting bracket or projecting block

QUOIN · cut-stone blocks along the edge of a building's doorway or corner

Second Empire Entrance with Pediment

This pediment appears to be a romanticized version of the kind of severe pediments seen in late Colonial, Federal, and Greek Revival entrances, with flattened cornices at the gable ends breaking the pitch and attenuating the entrance's welcome. Applied bolection molding was used to form a soft, rounded arch in the eave. Also of interest are the half pilasters with guttae, or pendant ornaments, on either side of the double doors.

The side view, to the left, shows the profile of the cresting and an Eastlake detail incised in the solid bracket.

STICK STYLE
1840 – 1876

This form of Victorian architecture had less complexity and fanciful ornamentation—and is less well known than Queen Anne style, which succeeded it in the late nineteenth century. The name refers to the decorative stickwork applied to outer walls—raised patterns of horizontal, vertical, or diagonal boards—and similar work found elsewhere on the exterior of otherwise basic, cross-gabled buildings. Unlike the more popular Queen Anne, Stick sought to proclaim, rather than hide, a house's inner framework in the tradition of medieval half-timbered construction.

To advocates of the style, the effect of a kind of "American basketry of the interior," as architectural historian Vincent J. Scully, Jr., noted of the exterior ornamentation, expressed a strength and truthfulness lacking in the previous two centuries, when versions of European architecture hid a house's frame. Stick houses' inner structures were also referenced by extending and exposing rafter ends under the wide overhangs, and by mixing numerous types of wood siding on the exterior walls.

As on other types of Victorian houses, a steep-gabled section of the one-story porch indicates the main entrance, which frequently is set off to one side rather than centered. The most distinctive feature of Stick facades and entrances is the use of decorative trusses under the gables of main and porch roofs, clearly marking both the center of the house and the porch steps, and giving houses the appearance of plain Swiss chalets. Along with brackets and braces, trusses appear in a variety of forms, including crosses, boxes, and fans.

Architect H. H. Richardson designed a number of buildings in the style, including his own house—Arrochar, on Staten Island, New York—in the late 1860s. Other fine examples include the Cram House in Middletown, Rhode Island, and St. Luke's Episcopal Church in Metuchen, New Jersey.

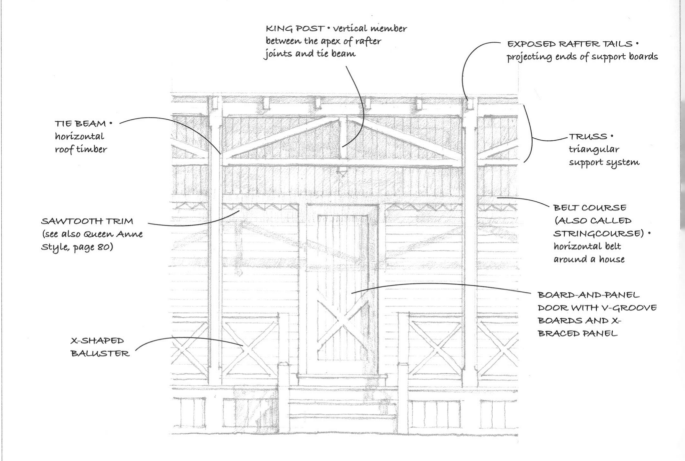

KING POST · vertical member between the apex of rafter joints and tie beam

EXPOSED RAFTER TAILS · projecting ends of support boards

TIE BEAM · horizontal roof timber

TRUSS · triangular support system

SAWTOOTH TRIM (see also Queen Anne Style, page 80)

BELT COURSE (ALSO CALLED STRINGCOURSE) · horizontal belt around a house

BOARD-AND-PANEL DOOR WITH V-GROOVE BOARDS AND X-BRACED PANEL

X-SHAPED BALUSTER

Stick Entrance

The essence of the Stick style was the use of decorative gable trusses, and applied stickwork to exterior walls, to represent the inner framework of the house. In other expressions of structural honesty, rafter ends were left exposed under wide eave overhangs, bracelike designs illustrated the point on porch balustrades and doors, and a variety of siding materials and styles was used at different levels of the facade.

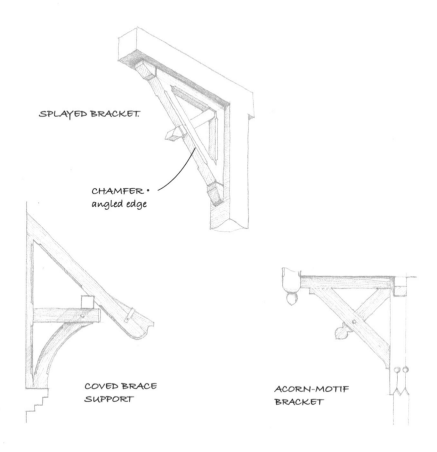

SPLAYED BRACKET.

CHAMFER ·
angled edge

COVED BRACE
SUPPORT

ACORN-MOTIF
BRACKET

Stick Brackets

The Stick style used decorative brackets such as these, as well as braces, trusses, and other devices, to represent the inner, structural integrity of the house, in the manner of medieval half-timbering, and were sometimes devoid of applied ornamentation.

QUEEN ANNE STYLE
1880 – 1910

Queen Anne is the architectural style that most people picture when they hear the words "Victorian house." Several themes and trends coincided to make the style wildly popular in this country in the last decades of the nineteenth century.

One factor was a fascination with what was perceived to be an "Old English" style of quaint buildings, based both on the English Queen Annes designed by British architect Richard Norman Shaw and on the temporary, half-timbered quarters for British officials at the Philadelphia Centennial Exposition of 1876. For Americans, the latter seemed to give rise to a certain romantic longing for home, which came during a period in which people were abandoning industrialized cities for the seaside and country (at least for the summers) and the imagined comforts of an earlier time.

The rambling informality of Queen Annes, and their eclectic mix of forms and building materials, filled the bill. The houses might combine any number of architectural elements: hipped roofs, gables, crossed gables, and conical roofs, usually at different levels; bay windows, towers, balconies, and upper-level porches; and a variety of exterior materials and details such as stone, different patterns of wood shingles, and gingerbread. Instead of painting the exteriors white, which had become the standard color of the American Colonial, architects and builders either left the wooden materials their natural colors or painted them in an array of earth tones.

The casualness of Queen Annes was amplified by full-width porches that wrapped around one or both sides of the houses, as well as one or more small sleeping porches off second-story bedrooms. Porch entrance stairways leading to the front door were framed in several ways: under flat roofs or rounded arches adorned with gingerbread or other woodwork; under gables decorated with gingerbread or brackets; or under a combination of the two. And, thanks to the Industrial Age, precut, mass-produced architectural details of the kind were available and affordable to carpenters across the country. The main doors themselves frequently featured similar, delicate designs in the woodwork and glass.

H. H. Richardson and an assistant, Stanford White (later a partner in the New York architectural firm McKim, Mead & White), are credited with designing the first Queen Anne house in America: the Watts-Sherman House in Newport, Rhode Island, in 1875. By the end of the Queen Annes' reign, they could be found from Maine to Texas, and Rhode Island to California, where, in the 1970s, the brightly colored "Painted Lady" Victorians in San Francisco's older neighborhoods became desirable again.

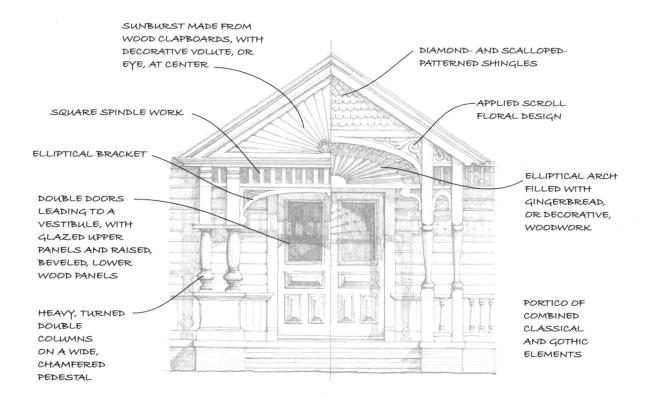

SUNBURST MADE FROM WOOD CLAPBOARDS, WITH DECORATIVE VOLUTE, OR EYE, AT CENTER

DIAMOND- AND SCALLOPED-PATTERNED SHINGLES

SQUARE SPINDLE WORK

APPLIED SCROLL FLORAL DESIGN

ELLIPTICAL BRACKET

ELLIPTICAL ARCH FILLED WITH GINGERBREAD, OR DECORATIVE, WOODWORK

DOUBLE DOORS LEADING TO A VESTIBULE, WITH GLAZED UPPER PANELS AND RAISED, BEVELED, LOWER WOOD PANELS

HEAVY, TURNED DOUBLE COLUMNS ON A WIDE, CHAMFERED PEDESTAL

PORTICO OF COMBINED CLASSICAL AND GOTHIC ELEMENTS

Queen Anne Entrance

Dominant gables facing the street and leading to sweeping porches made abundantly clear the way in. Invariably, they were framed and supported by turned posts and decorative brackets, and filled with gingerbread and patterned wood shingles. Above, on the right, paired posts support a gable of highly intricate and visible ornamentation: a fan-shaped arch of turned spindles, scroll filigree brackets, and diamond- and scallop-shaped shingles in the upper eaves. On the left, an elliptical bracket underlies square spindle work and, in the eave, a sunburst pattern of clapboard spun out from a central volute.

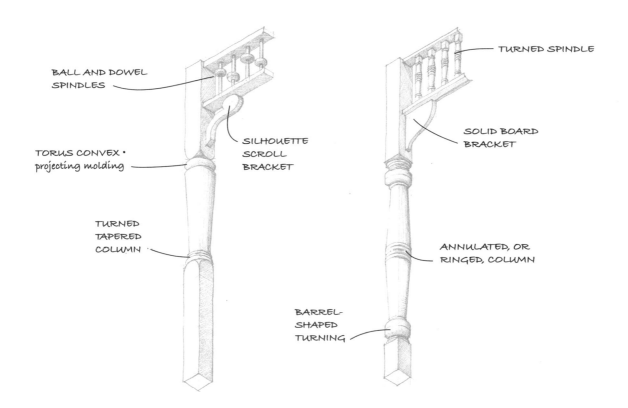

BALL AND DOWEL
SPINDLES

TORUS CONVEX •
projecting molding

TURNED
TAPERED
COLUMN

SILHOUETTE
SCROLL
BRACKET

TURNED SPINDLE

SOLID BOARD
BRACKET

ANNULATED, OR
RINGED, COLUMN

BARREL-
SHAPED
TURNING

Queen Anne Posts and Spindle Work

Instead of being carved by hand as in the past, Victorian porch posts, columns, and
ornamental woodwork were mass-produced in mills, making them abundant and
affordable, and able to be precut and shipped anywhere in the country. Posts and spindles
such as these were turned on a lathe, a machine that shapes wood by holding and rapidly
turning it against the edge of a fixed cutting tool.

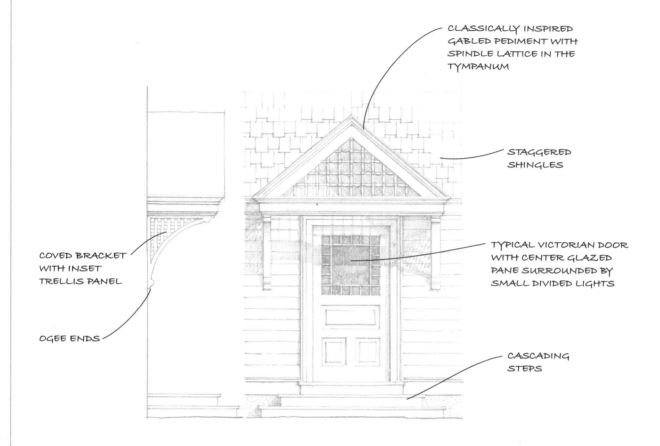

CLASSICALLY INSPIRED
GABLED PEDIMENT WITH
SPINDLE LATTICE IN THE
TYMPANUM

STAGGERED
SHINGLES

TYPICAL VICTORIAN DOOR
WITH CENTER GLAZED
PANE SURROUNDED BY
SMALL DIVIDED LIGHTS

COVED BRACKET
WITH INSET
TRELLIS PANEL

OGEE ENDS

CASCADING
STEPS

Queen Anne Entrance with Portico

Even modest Queen Anne doorways (typically back and side entrances, or front entrances to outbuildings) were embellished in the Victorian style. Above, the gable eave of spindle lattice is repeated in the staggered shingling and in the small divided lights surrounding the upper panel of glass—a familiar pattern in glazed Queen Anne doors.

In the left-hand illustration, a coved bracket with an inset of trellis pine softens the hard lines of the classically inspired gable roof.

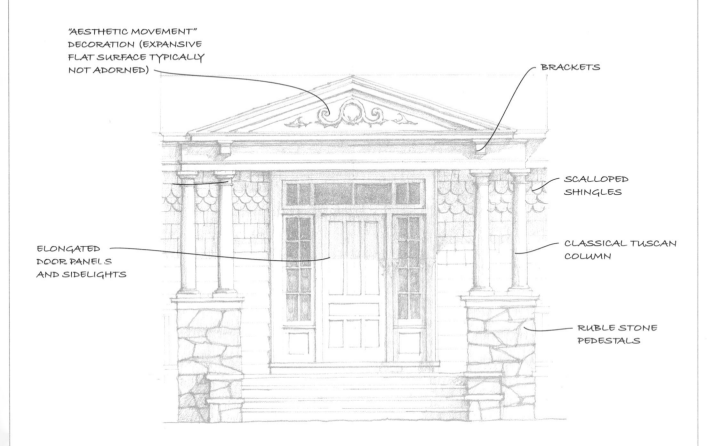

"AESTHETIC MOVEMENT" DECORATION (EXPANSIVE FLAT SURFACE TYPICALLY NOT ADORNED)

BRACKETS

SCALLOPED SHINGLES

ELONGATED DOOR PANELS AND SIDELIGHTS

CLASSICAL TUSCAN COLUMN

RUBLE STONE PEDESTALS

Queen Anne (Free Classical) Entrance

This entrance illustrates the transition from Queen Anne- to Shingle-style houses. The solid door with elongated panels, sidelights, and plain transom recalls the late Colonial period. Oddly, for a style moving forward into the twentieth century, it makes use of a couple of classical details: tapered Tuscan columns and a festoonlike ornament in the tympanum that, while not untypical of Queen Anne houses, is also found in Greek Revival entrances.

SHINGLE STYLE
1880 – 1910; 1990 –

Near the end of the nineteenth century and America's intense but short love affair with Queen Annes, architects began to reassemble the bones of the period's various house styles—large masses and irregular shapes, complex roof layouts, big porches—and wrap them in a smooth, uniform, unembellished skin. The idea was that an unornamented and unbroken surface of natural cedar shingles would offset the frivolity and showiness of the Victorian styles, creating more rustic, rambling vacation homes of the kind New England coastal settlers might have built.

The meandering layouts of Shingle houses suited an increasingly open American lifestyle. Of course, there was more to the architecture than function. The use of largely uniform wood shingles represented a nostalgia for seventeenth-century New England Capes and Saltboxes. At the same time, the Shingle style signaled a further Americanization of the Queen Anne, which it quickly began replacing as a popular style for not only huge country and seaside "cottages" for rich city dwellers but wholly new and original American residences in the late nineteenth century. And, inasmuch as the wooden skin completely concealed the frame of the house, it was a total rejection of the concept of the Stick style of several decades earlier.

Still, it's easy to perceive earlier architectural styles, especially Queen Anne, under many of the shingled surfaces. In a similar way, Shingle-style entrances can be seen as bulked-up versions of Queen Anne porch entries. They are characterized by rounded, wood-clad Romanesque arches that are usually positioned in the center of deep porches and supported by thick columns. Though the piers are often constructed of rough stone, the columns tend to be wrapped in shingles. In keeping with the horizontal nature of many Shingle-style houses and porches, the size of the archways and doors tends to be wide, though not especially elaborate.

Architect William Ralph Emerson's house, which he designed for himself and his family in Mount Desert, Maine, in 1879, was one of the first Shingle-style buildings. McKim, Mead & White's Edna Villa, in Newport, Rhode Island, remains one of the best examples of the style. The largest Shingle building, and the farthest afield from its New England source, is the Hotel del Coronado in San Diego, California.

In the 1990s, a second wave of Shingle-style design in the Northeast, in particular along the Long Island shore, produced Shingle houses more massive and rambling than those built a century ago.

BOWED AND SHINGLED
ROOF SKIRT OVER THE
WINDOWS

FLARED EAVE,
OR OVERHANG

DOUBLE
TIMBER
COLUMN

COVED BRACKET
(see also page 69)

COUPLING
TIMBER ·
horizontal member
connecting
columns or posts

SASH AND PANEL
(WINDOW FRAME)
DOOR

Shingle House

The rambling Shingle "cottages" built along the New England coast in the late nineteenth
and early twentieth centuries expressed informality that was in stark contrast to the
high ornamentalism of the Queen Anne style. Roomy entrance porches featured heavy
timbered posts and brackets, matching the medievallike mass of the houses themselves.
In this drawing, note the flared porch roof and bowed roof skirt over the second-floor
band of windows.

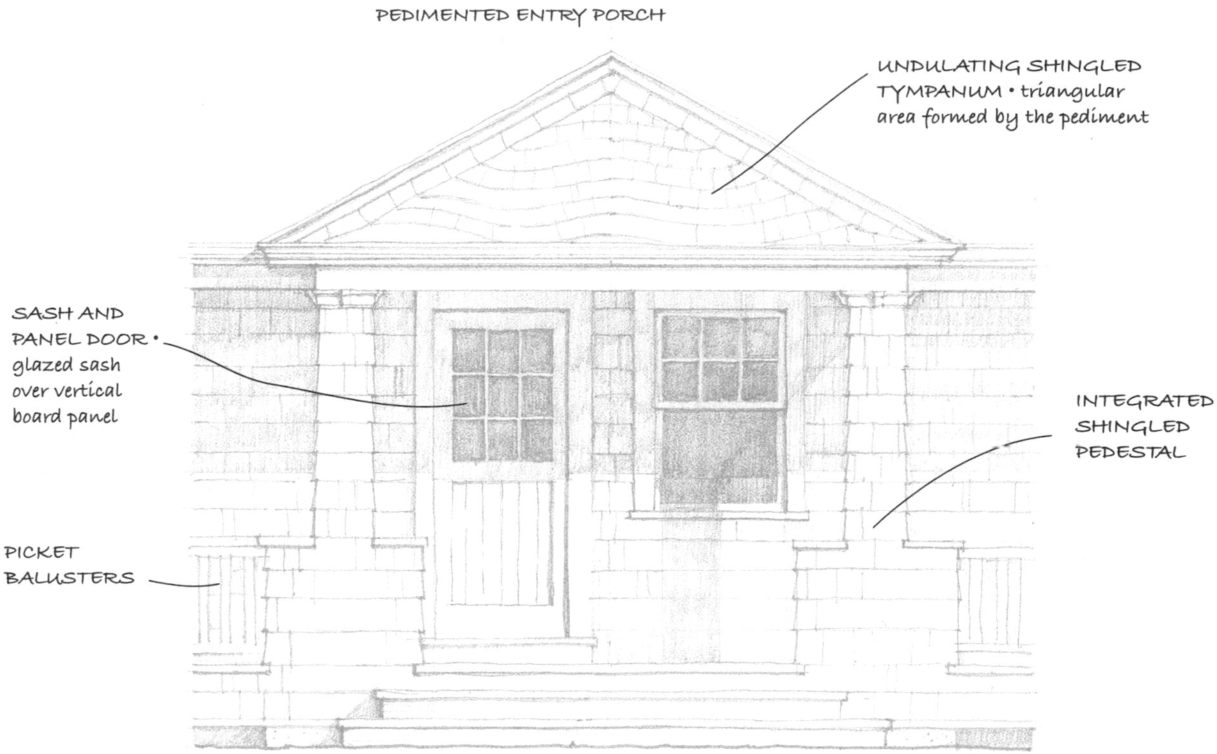

PEDIMENTED ENTRY PORCH

UNDULATING SHINGLED
TYMPANUM · triangular
area formed by the pediment

SASH AND
PANEL DOOR ·
glazed sash
over vertical
board panel

INTEGRATED
SHINGLED
PEDESTAL

PICKET
BALUSTERS

Shingle Entrance

The siding is both the style and the ornamentation in Shingle houses. The unbroken skin of shingles, or shakes, which were left unpainted to weather to a silvery brown, was meant to convey a rustic informality. Nearly every part of the facade was clad in shingles, including porch piers and posts, and gabled pediment and trim.

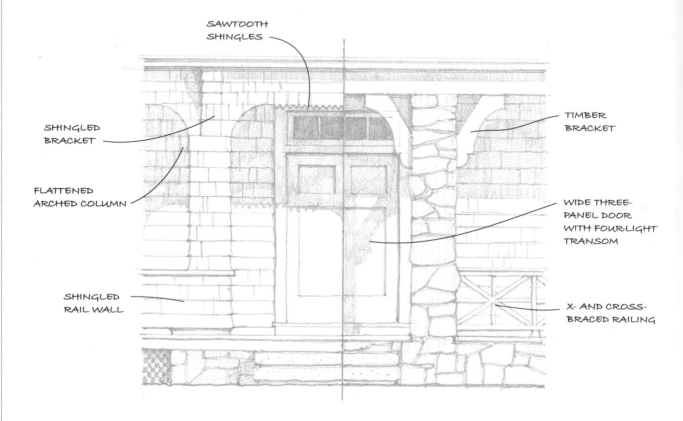

SAWTOOTH
SHINGLES

SHINGLED
BRACKET

FLATTENED
ARCHED COLUMN

SHINGLED
RAIL WALL

TIMBER
BRACKET

WIDE THREE-
PANEL DOOR
WITH FOUR-LIGHT
TRANSOM

X- AND CROSS-
BRACED RAILING

Shingle Arch and Door

In this drawing, the broad, flattened entry arch—part of an arcade of arches on the porch—and the wide door with four-light transom follow the general profile of Shingle-style houses and reflect the influence of Richardsonian Romanesque architecture (see pages 92–97). On the right, the porch post is a continuation of the fieldstone foundation, a rustic touch. On the left, the rail wall, post, arches, and fascia (board under the eaves) are sheathed in shingle to create the impression of a uniform, nearly seamless exterior.

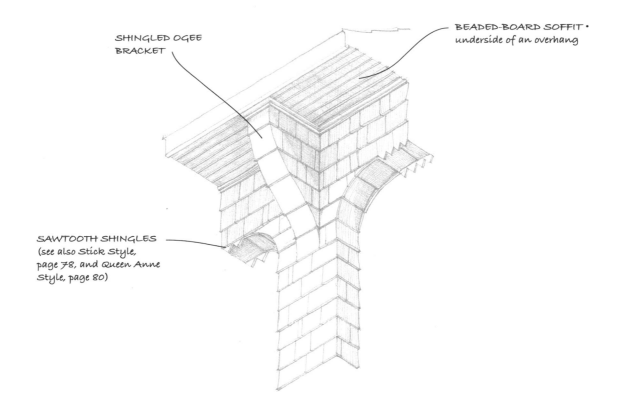

SHINGLED OGEE BRACKET

BEADED-BOARD SOFFIT •
underside of an overhang

SAWTOOTH SHINGLES
(see also Stick Style,
page 78, and Queen Anne
Style, page 80)

Shingle-Style Column and Bracket

The idea of a smooth, uniform skin sheathing Shingle-style houses extended even to columns and brackets. Here the ogee, or S-shaped, bracket appears to support the roof overhang, but it is largely decorative. The soffit, or underside of the overhang, is beaded board rather than a single width of wood for a casual, rustic look that is representative of the style.

RICHARDSONIAN ROMANESQUE STYLE
1880 – 1900

If you've seen buildings designed in the Richardsonian Romanesque style, you've glimpsed the Middle Ages — specifically, that period when churches throughout Europe expanded to accommodate their many worshippers, adding massive stone walls, vaults, flying buttresses, and thick rounded arches to those structures.

A Romanesque Revival movement in the early nineteenth century resulted in hulking public buildings, such as the original Smithsonian Institution, completed in Washington, D.C., in 1855. (Romanesque Revival was also referred to as Round Style, or Lombard, after the medieval architecture of the Lombardy region of northern Italy.) Yet it wasn't until the last two decades of the century that it was fully Americanized by Boston architect Henry Hobson Richardson, who had been a leading designer of impressive Second Empire, Queen Anne, and Shingle homes for well-to-do clients.

Richardson refined and redefined the style, employing French and English details and, more important, his own sensibilities. So strongly did he shape Romanesque elements to his personality and tastes, in fact, that he is inextricably identified with the style, which became the first choice for public buildings during the late 1800s. Richardson (who, coincidentally, weighed three hundred pounds) favored horizontal stone buildings of great mass and solidity, many of them enhanced by towers or turrets. In a sense, they were muscular, masonry versions of Queen Anne structures.

The major difference between the Romanesque Revival of the 1840s and the Richardsonian movement is the rough-cut exterior masonry walls that were offset, in the arches and sometimes bands, by different textured and colored stones. In addition, Richardson's were simple, more rambling compositions than the earlier buildings.

While the buildings are meant to be picturesque, they also preach permanence. The hallmarks of the style are windows and doorways deeply recessed behind big, rounded arches or arcades, usually resting on squat piers or columns. The surrounds are composed of high, shaped stones of different textures and colors, which, again, offset the heaviness of the facades and openings. Doors also tend to be broad, heavy, and rounded, mirroring the arches.

Richardson worked on a wide range of religious, public, and academic campus buildings in the 1870s and 1880s: Trinity Church in Boston, the Allegheny County courthouse and jail in Pittsburgh, Sever Hall at Harvard, the Marshall Field store in Chicago, and the Hartford, Connecticut, train station, among others. Along with those buildings, and a good number of Shingle-style commissions, he also designed a handful of private residences. One of his most famous is the Glessner House in Chicago—a massive granite structure likened, by one critic of the day, to an armory.

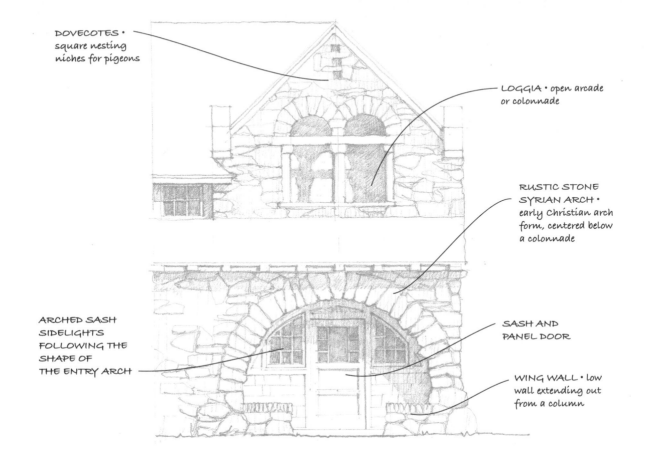

DOVECOTES • square nesting niches for pigeons

LOGGIA • open arcade or colonnade

RUSTIC STONE SYRIAN ARCH • early Christian arch form, centered below a colonnade

ARCHED SASH SIDELIGHTS FOLLOWING THE SHAPE OF THE ENTRY ARCH

SASH AND PANEL DOOR

WING WALL • low wall extending out from a column

Richardsonian Romanesque Entrance and Windows

American architect H. H. Richardson's interpretation of Roman and Byzantine elements produced, in the late nineteenth century, a limited number of stone mansions that were unlike any other residences in North America. Their most distinguishing features were recessed windows and doorways announced by massive rounded arches of rough-cut stone. The entrance arches either began at ground level, where they might sprout wing walls, or sat on piers. Doors could be massive, rounded, and paneled, or more traditionally Victorian, as in this drawing.

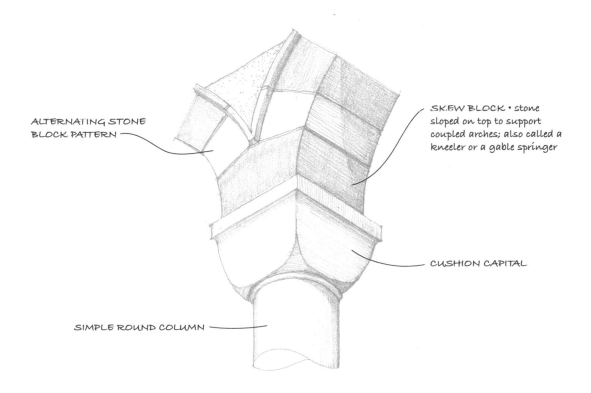

ALTERNATING STONE
BLOCK PATTERN

SKEW BLOCK • stone
sloped on top to support
coupled arches; also called a
kneeler or a gable springer

CUSHION CAPITAL

SIMPLE ROUND COLUMN

Richardsonian Romanesque Capital and Arch

Richardson also drew on eleventh-century Romanesque forms—massive stone walls and arcades of rounded arches—for the style of public buildings and private mansions that came to bear his name. He borrowed cushion capitals from Norman architecture (the French Romanesque style) and alternated colors and types of masonry, as the capital and arch bases in this drawing show.

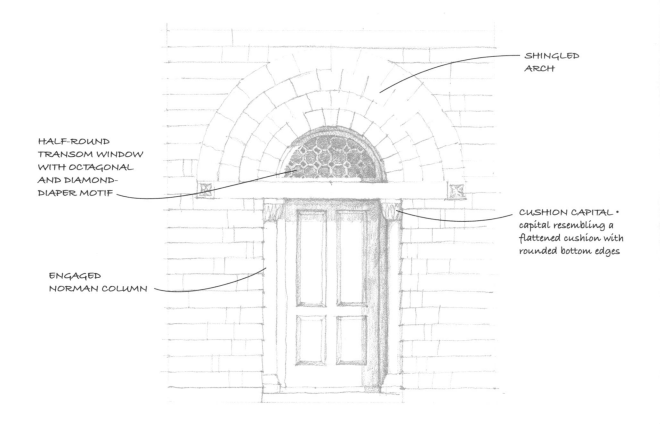

SHINGLED ARCH

HALF-ROUND TRANSOM WINDOW WITH OCTAGONAL AND DIAMOND-DIAPER MOTIF

CUSHION CAPITAL • capital resembling a flattened cushion with rounded bottom edges

ENGAGED NORMAN COLUMN

Shingled Richardsonian Romanesque Entrance

More public buildings than houses were built in the Richardsonian Romanesque style; masonry mansions cost a great deal more than wood Queen Annes, for one thing, and Richardson's death at forty-eight preempted more residential commissions. But he also designed a number of Shingle residences, and the entrance shown above is a shingled abstraction of the Romanesque style. The treatment, however, places it more firmly within the Victorian period. The big shingled arch over the half-round transom and door is a representation in wood of Richardsonian Romanesque stone arches.

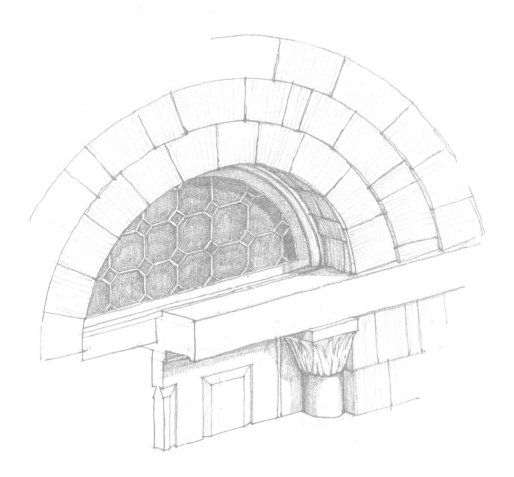

Half-Round Transom Window and Cushion Capital

Half-round windows aren't usually so deeply recessed, but the one in this design has to visually carry the broad arch and the mass of the rest of the facade. The pattern of the glass is more Eastern than Western European. The floral design of the cushion capitals is Roman and Byzantine.

ECLECTIC PERIOD

1890 – 1940

TUDOR REVIVAL STYLE
1890 – 1940

The first imitations of a traditional architectural type are usually closest to the original and designed for a privileged few. This was true of the elaborate Tudor mansions built in America around the turn of the nineteenth century. Drawing on a number of English forms—sixteenth-century Tudor, Elizabethan, Jacobean—they incorporated steep-pitched roofs, massive chimneys, tall windows of leaded glass, and a mix of brick, stone, stucco, or wood cladding.

The Tudor houses most suburban dwellers probably know, however, are Tudor Revivals, prototypical development houses that were popular and widespread in the 1920s and 1930s. In addition to the earlier forms mentioned, all sorts of other historical periods and styles—Medieval, Renaissance, Gothic, Craftsman—were likely to be represented in Tudor Revival houses. They simply were refitted into a popular, commercial substyle for middle-class urban and suburban developments, with the dream of ownership practically as easy as ordering a prefab kit by mail. These may have been playhouses compared with the late-nineteenth- and early-twentieth-century mansions—the half-timbering is decorative, not structural—but they were picturesque, comfortable, and affordable.

Whether or not they are historically correct, the front entrances manage to look impressively English. The doorways are set in half-timbered gables that are bumped out a foot or more from the front wall. Occasionally, too, the doorways will show masonry surrounds with brick or quoinlike stones integrated into the material, along with Tudor arches. Doors, carved or batten style, are usually rounded, substantial looking (even on very small houses), and inviting.

Tudor Revival houses are readily identifiable by a number of elements rarely seen together in other types of residential buildings: steep roof pitches, half-timber work, narrow windows of leaded glass, and a mix of brick, stone, stucco, or wood on the facade.

Historically, Tudor grew out of the Gothic style that swept Western Europe between the twelfth and sixteenth centuries (it's named after Henry VII of England, whose family name was Tudor). When talking about Tudor homes in this country, we generally mean the mansions of the early decades of the twentieth century, which were closely modeled on English Tudor, Elizabethan, or Jacobean styles, but also Tudor Revival period houses, which were popular and widespread during the 1920s and 1930s.

These are less a pure architectural style than an eclectic blend of late–medieval English elements and details, and often faux elements and details at that. While in England half-timbers, an identifying Tudor feature, were usually structural, in this country and in these houses, they are mostly ornamental. Although vaguely modeled on basic medieval structures, the point was to reference a distant and supposedly cozy historical experience, while providing the comforts and conveniences of a twentieth-century American home.

The result was suburban and exurban developments of affordable Tudoresque houses in many metropolitan areas (in some areas, houses in the style were called Stockbroker Tudor). The style also showed up in half-timbered facades on apartment complexes and community buildings.

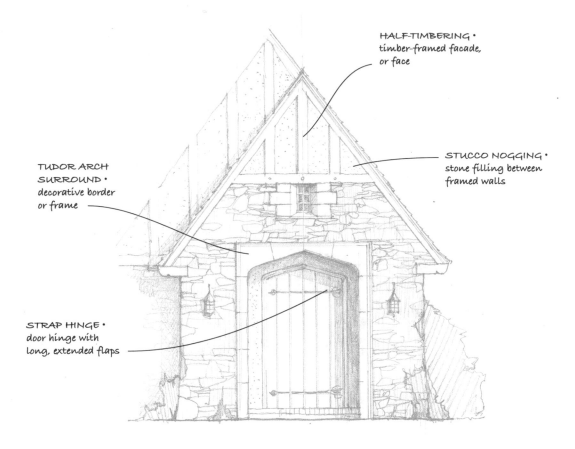

HALF-TIMBERING •
timber-framed facade,
or face

STUCCO NOGGING •
stone filling between
framed walls

**TUDOR ARCH
SURROUND** •
decorative border
or frame

STRAP HINGE •
door hinge with
long, extended flaps

Tudor Revival Entrance

In the early twentieth century, American interpretations of medieval English buildings produced Tudor Revival houses that more or less accurately copied the original style and its variations. The earliest examples were mansions with projecting, front-facing gables. These gables created interior space for foyers and, more important, set the stage for prominent, immediately recognizable Tudor doors: broad batten or paneled doors with Tudor arches and elongated wrought-iron hinges set in limestone or other masonry surrounds.

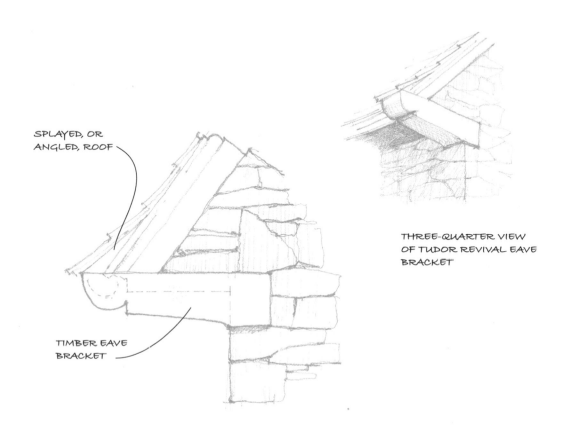

SPLAYED, OR
ANGLED, ROOF

THREE-QUARTER VIEW
OF TUDOR REVIVAL EAVE
BRACKET

TIMBER EAVE
BRACKET

Tudor Revival Eave Bracket

This timber bracket serves two purposes: It finishes the eave with a solid form, befitting the Tudor style, and it caps and hides the rain gutter. The splayed shingle covers only the end of the bracket.

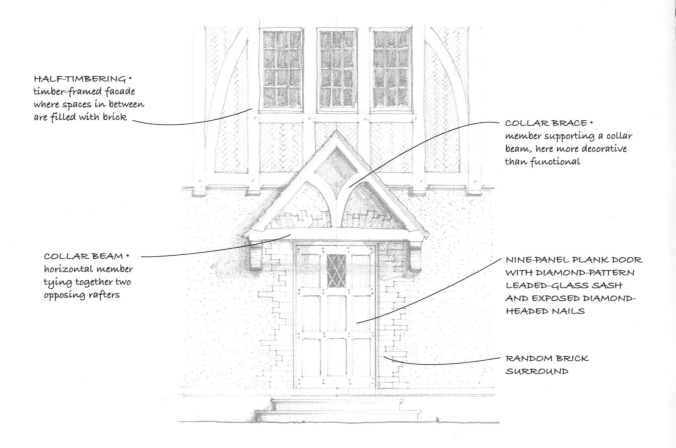

HALF-TIMBERING · timber-framed facade where spaces in between are filled with brick

COLLAR BRACE · member supporting a collar beam, here more decorative than functional

COLLAR BEAM · horizontal member tying together two opposing rafters

NINE-PANEL PLANK DOOR WITH DIAMOND-PATTERN LEADED-GLASS SASH AND EXPOSED DIAMOND-HEADED NAILS

RANDOM BRICK SURROUND

Tudor Revival Entrance with Portico

Although the second-story window surround in this drawing is elaborate, more modest Tudor Revival houses, which crowded metropolitan suburban developments in the 1920s and 1930s, set doorways in porticoes rather than full gable projections. Brick and stone, or stone veneer, were frequently integrated into exterior stucco walls. Half-timbering in the gable eave and window surround, with masonry nogging, or filling, approximated the look, if not the function, of medieval Tudor timber-frame construction.

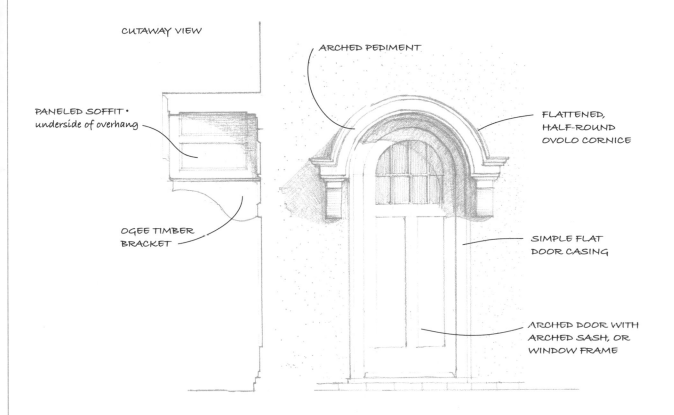

CUTAWAY VIEW

ARCHED PEDIMENT

PANELED SOFFIT •
underside of overhang

FLATTENED,
HALF-ROUND
OVOLO CORNICE

OGEE TIMBER
BRACKET

SIMPLE FLAT
DOOR CASING

ARCHED DOOR WITH
ARCHED SASH, OR
WINDOW FRAME

Tudor Revival Entrance with Pediment

A simple arched pediment frames a rounded door that is more Renaissance than Tudor, although Tudor Revival houses drew on many medieval styles and details. This doorway would be appropriate for smaller houses and cottages. In the left-hand illustration, from the side, the thick ogee timber bracket appears formidable, in keeping with the general intent of Tudor entrances and facades.

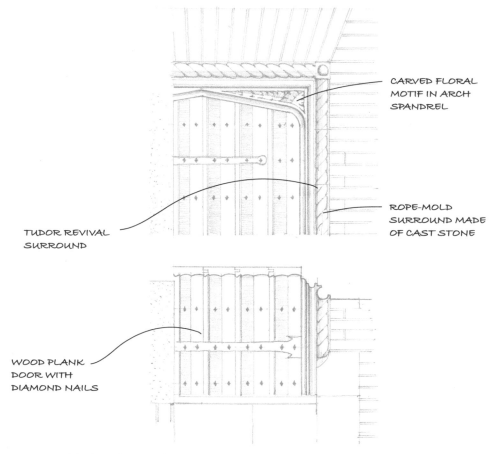

CARVED FLORAL
MOTIF IN ARCH
SPANDREL

ROPE-MOLD
SURROUND MADE
OF CAST STONE

TUDOR REVIVAL
SURROUND

WOOD PLANK
DOOR WITH
DIAMOND NAILS

Tudor Revival Doors, Surrounds, and Hinge Straps

Tudor Revival entrance surrounds often featured stone, either cut block or precast ornamental concrete, such as this spandrel with a floral decoration framed with narrow rope molding in the top drawing. The four-centered arch door (the arch is derived from the intersecting lines of four different compass points), with its tongue-and-groove design and diamond-headed nails, is typically Tudor. In the drawings on the opposite page, oversize strap hinges made of cast iron reinforce the idea of a grand and massive entrance.

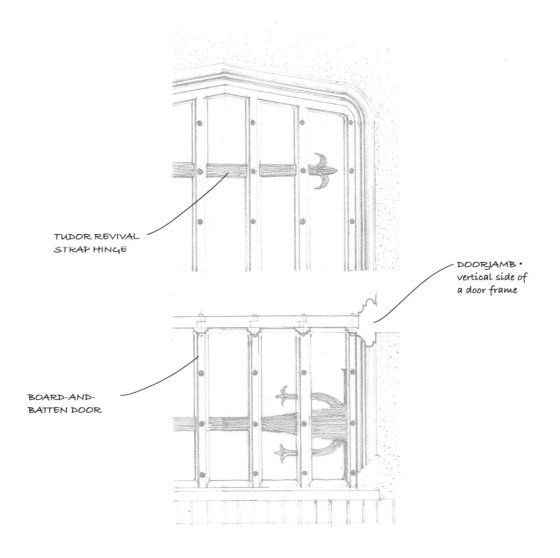

TUDOR REVIVAL
STRAP HINGE

BOARD-AND-
BATTEN DOOR

DOORJAMB ·
vertical side of
a door frame

MISSION STYLE
1890 – 1910

Following nearly a century of stylistic crossbreeding in the creation of American hybrid houses, architects at the turn of the nineteenth century devoted themselves to more or less faithful reproductions of period home design. One of the most widespread and enduring of these was the Mission style.

Long before the British settled the Northeast, Spain colonized the Gulf and Southeastern coasts. Spain's major and lasting influence on American architecture can be seen in the Mission buildings that spread throughout California and across the Southwest in the late nineteenth and early twentieth centuries. A substyle of Spanish Colonial Revival houses, the Southwestern Mission style was considered the California equivalent of Colonial Revival houses in the Northeast.

If the squat porch columns and wide, rounded arches seem reminiscent of those on Romanesque buildings, it may be because both styles have roots in ancient Roman architecture. Mission houses also drew details from the Spanish missionary churches built in California in the late eighteenth century.

Mission entrances are free of moldings and the kinds of ornamentation found in much of American residential architecture. What typically distinguishes them is a broad central arch that opens into an airy entry porch. The arch is usually capped, either at porch roof or main roof level, with a parapet—a low, thick wall or solid railing at the edge of a porch or main roof—that is shaped and curvilinear. By contrast, the wood doors are heavy but unembellished.

Aside from appearing in private residences throughout California and the Southwest, Mission was also a popular design for hotels, such as the Golden Gate Park Lodge in San Francisco, built in 1896, and the Alvarado Hotel in Albuquerque, New Mexico, finished in 1905. One of the best examples of public Mission buildings is the courthouse in Santa Barbara, California.

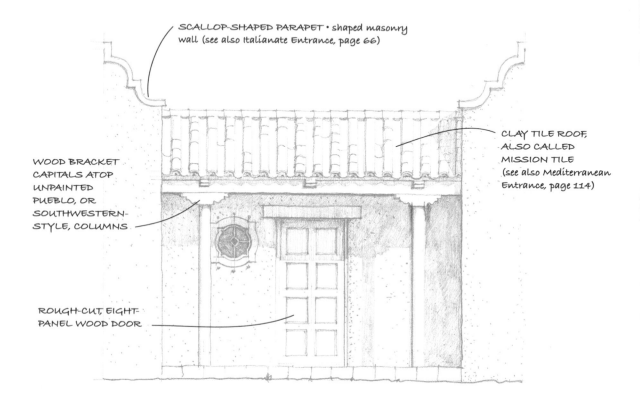

SCALLOP-SHAPED PARAPET · shaped masonry wall (see also Italianate Entrance, page 66)

CLAY TILE ROOF, ALSO CALLED MISSION TILE (see also Mediterranean Entrance, page 114)

WOOD BRACKET CAPITALS ATOP UNPAINTED PUEBLO, OR SOUTHWESTERN-STYLE, COLUMNS

ROUGH-CUT, EIGHT-PANEL WOOD DOOR

Mission Entrance

Spain's influence on American architecture can still be seen today, centuries after the last Spanish outpost dissapeared. In the early twentieth century, Mission-style churches, public buildings, and houses spread from southern California and the Southwest to Florida and the Northeast. Their Mediterranean and Roman roots were clearly evident: red pantile roofs, stucco walls, deep porches and arcades of natural round timbers, and plain wood doors with little ornamentation.

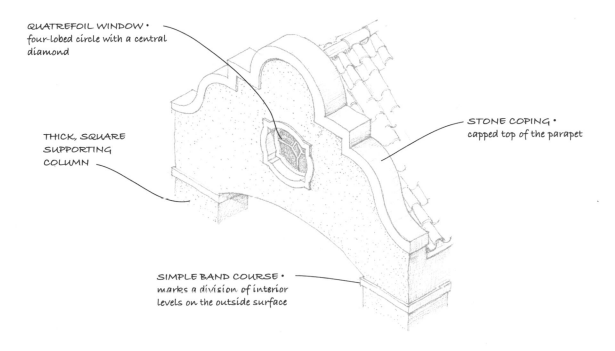

QUATREFOIL WINDOW ·
four-lobed circle with a central
diamond

THICK, SQUARE
SUPPORTING
COLUMN

STONE COPING ·
capped top of the parapet

SIMPLE BAND COURSE ·
marks a division of interior
levels on the outside surface

Mission Parapet

Mission roofs and dormers were often edged with parapets—low walls rising above roof level and usually scallop-shaped—to enhance and ornament the flat, unembellished facades and give the low, squat buildings more vertical presence. Some parapets also featured small quatrefoil windows such as that pictured above.

MEDITERRANEAN STYLE
1920 – 1940

In the 1920s, another residential design began rolling across the country, not from the proper and chilly Northeast, where so many preceding architectural styles had originated, but from California and Florida, two states on opposite shores. By the 1940s, it had spread to the Southwest.

Mediterranean style, which replaced Mission style in the public's imagination, was most popular in California, New Mexico, and Arizona, and in Florida, all of which shared similar climates, light, and ambience. The style suggested sunshine and health, historical context and newness, and glamour and attractiveness, especially to Northerners. More so than the Mission style, it drew from a wide base of influences: Mexican and Spanish, and also North African, Italian, and Greek. Its main developments were the use of an arcaded loggia in front of the house, which served as an open entrance porch, and a palette of Mediterranean colors: white- or cream-colored walls, orange or red roofs, sea-blue ceilings and trim. Mediterranean houses are typically simpler than Spanish Colonial houses, with less exterior ornamentation and more straightforward lines, but they are more elaborate and elegant than Mission houses.

In California, Hollywood magnates and movie stars commissioned mansions modeled loosely on traditional seaside Mediterranean architecture (the most famous of them is San Simeon, William Randolph Hearst's eclectic Spanish Renaissance castle in California). These huge houses typically featured semicircular terra-cotta Mission tiles, or S-shaped Spanish tiles, over flat, low-pitched gable- or hipped-roof lines; brick or thick stucco walls, which were frequently painted white for contrast with the red roof tiles; shuttered windows; and ornate wrought-iron grillwork. In some Mediterranean-style houses, doors are arched and paneled, with a small shaped window and a second-floor balcony directly overhead.

In the mid-1920s, Addison Mizner and other architects were helping popularize the style in Florida. One of the most famous Mediterranean-style residences is Mar-a-Lago, built for cereal heiress Marjorie Merriweather Post and now a Trump resort and spa.

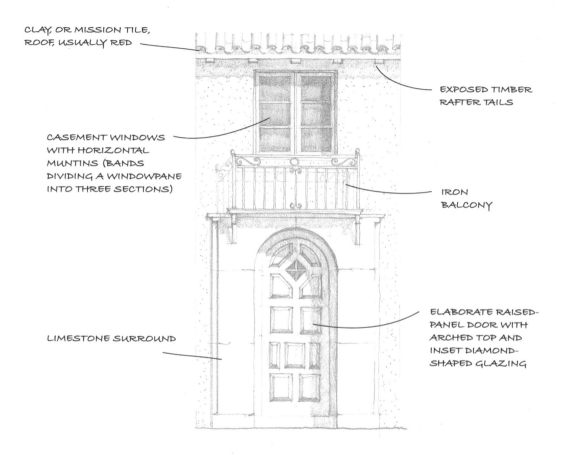

CLAY, OR MISSION TILE, ROOF, USUALLY RED

EXPOSED TIMBER RAFTER TAILS

CASEMENT WINDOWS WITH HORIZONTAL MUNTINS (BANDS DIVIDING A WINDOWPANE INTO THREE SECTIONS)

IRON BALCONY

ELABORATE RAISED-PANEL DOOR WITH ARCHED TOP AND INSET DIAMOND-SHAPED GLAZING

LIMESTONE SURROUND

Mediterranean Entrance

Although they share origins and materials with Mission buildings, Mediterranean-style houses of the 1920s are usually larger and grander—many were considered mansions, then and now—with more decorative detail (though still a far cry from Georgian or Victorian houses). Doors are often arched, and some are inset with small shaped windows. In the finest examples of the style, the doorways themselves are set in surrounds of large stone blocks and highlighted by overhead casement windows and balconies with wrought-iron railings.

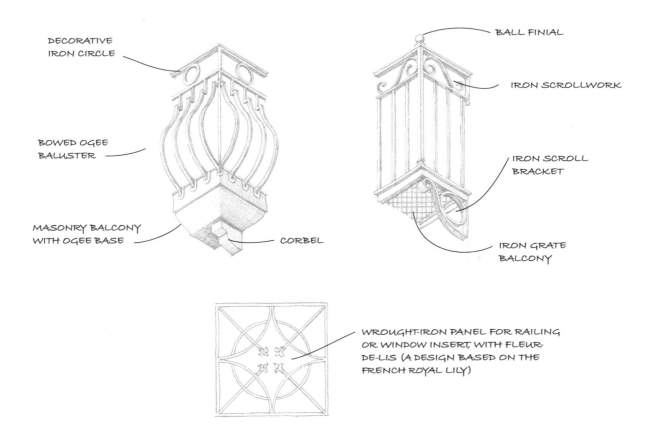

DECORATIVE
IRON CIRCLE

BOWED OGEE
BALUSTER

MASONRY BALCONY
WITH OGEE BASE

CORBEL

BALL FINIAL

IRON SCROLLWORK

IRON SCROLL
BRACKET

IRON GRATE
BALCONY

WROUGHT-IRON PANEL FOR RAILING
OR WINDOW INSERT, WITH FLEUR-
DE-LIS (A DESIGN BASED ON THE
FRENCH ROYAL LILY)

Mediterranean Ironwork Variations

Wrought iron was used in decorative railings for balconies, as well as window grilles, lanterns, hinges, and door knobs, in Mediterranean houses. The ironwork designs, which were relatively restrained, drew upon a sea of influences: Spanish Classical, Italian Renaissance, Moorish, and Byzantine.

ARTS AND CRAFTS PERIOD
1895 – 1930

PRAIRIE STYLE
1895 – 1920

The suburban American streetscape changed forever when Frank Lloyd Wright, and the group of Chicago architects known collectively as the Prairie School, began designing low, horizontal, open floor–plan houses across the Midwest in the years around the turn of the nineteenth century.

Like the Greene brothers in California (see page 122), Wright was influenced by Japanese design as well as by the idea of "organic" architecture: houses designed in harmony with their setting and function that complement, rather than compete with, the natural beauty of the landscape by being well integrated into their sites.

Prairie-style buildings are usually two-story rectangles with projecting, one-story wings; low hipped roofs with wide overhangs; and banks of windows that bring light into the interior, provide sweeping views of the outdoors, and accentuate the horizontality of the design. The houses' low profiles fit with the flat Midwestern landscape. Their open floor plans grew out of a reaction to the small, closed-off rooms of early-nineteenth-century styles, particularly Victorian.

At the same time, though their Prairie houses lack the overt ornamentation of earlier styles, Wright and other architects incorporated geometric designs in stained-glass windows, doors, and interior room dividers and have become synonymous with the style. The buildings are usually faced with brick, smooth stucco, or plaster, or a combination of these materials.

The one-story front entrance porches of Prairie-style houses are also low and broad and made prominent by thick square posts and generous, often recessed gables. (In some Wright-designed houses, however, the main entrance is secluded and hidden from public view.) Front doors might feature one of a number of arrangements of square and/or rectangular panes of clear or stained glass. Usually, a door design, based on designs found in nature, mirrored the patterns found in a house's windows.

Among the Prairie masterpieces created by Frank Lloyd Wright and his associates are the 1901 Willits House in Highland Park, Illinois; the J. K. Ingalls House in Oak Park, Illinois, designed in 1909; the 1904 Martin House in Buffalo, New York; and the Robie House in Chicago, completed in 1909.

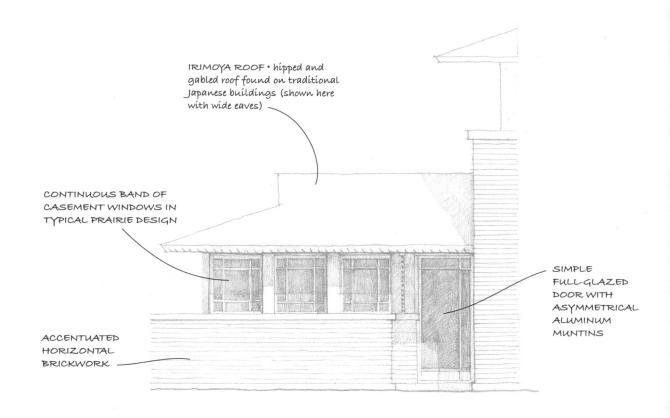

IRIMOYA ROOF • hipped and gabled roof found on traditional Japanese buildings (shown here with wide eaves)

CONTINUOUS BAND OF CASEMENT WINDOWS IN TYPICAL PRAIRIE DESIGN

SIMPLE FULL-GLAZED DOOR WITH ASYMMETRICAL ALUMINUM MUNTINS

ACCENTUATED HORIZONTAL BRICKWORK

Prairie Entrance

Typically associated with Frank Lloyd Wright and built throughout the Midwest between 1900 and 1920, Prairie-style houses emphasized a connection to the land with its long, low wings and porches with band windows. The style spawned the Ranch house in the 1950s and 1960s. Although entrances were frequently hidden under wide plain eaves, Prairie doors with full panels of glass and minimal ornamentation celebrated a new openness to the landscape.

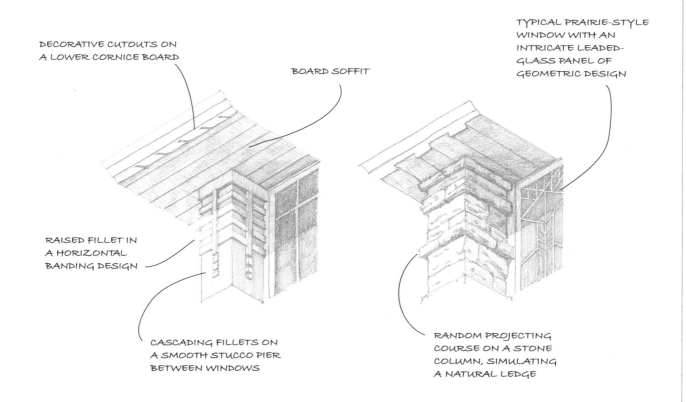

DECORATIVE CUTOUTS ON
A LOWER CORNICE BOARD

BOARD SOFFIT

TYPICAL PRAIRIE-STYLE
WINDOW WITH AN
INTRICATE LEADED-
GLASS PANEL OF
GEOMETRIC DESIGN

RAISED FILLET IN
A HORIZONTAL
BANDING DESIGN

CASCADING FILLETS ON
A SMOOTH STUCCO PIER
BETWEEN WINDOWS

RANDOM PROJECTING
COURSE ON A STONE
COLUMN, SIMULATING
A NATURAL LEDGE

Prairie Piers and Glazing Variations

Frank Lloyd Wright's interest in creating organic architecture extended from the low, horizontal profile of the model Prairie-style house to minute details in wood, stone, and glass. The thick piers on which wide roof overhangs rested were frequently banded with projecting courses of wood or stone, simulating natural cascades of ledge rock.

Glazing in the doors and windows took a number of forms, from designs found in nature to geometric shapes: squares, rectangles, triangles, and parallelograms.

CRAFTSMAN/BUNGALOW STYLE
1905 – 1930

This style derived its name from house designs published in *The Craftsman,* an influential magazine produced under the direction of architect and designer Gustav Stickely. It was Stickely's "mission" (hence the Mission furniture he designed) to try to teach average Americans good design. But the Craftsman style is perhaps most identified with its main practitioners, Charles Sumner Greene and Henry Mather Greene, brothers and partners in the California architectural design firm Greene & Greene. Also influenced by Japanese architecture, and by William Morris and the Arts and Crafts movement in England at the end of the nineteenth century, the Greene brothers designed or inspired high-style Craftsman bungalows from the early 1900s to the 1930s.

Craftsman bungalows and houses are characterized by the use of natural materials and colors—a bungalow is "a house reduced to its simplest form," Stickley wrote, and natural enough in appearance to blend into any landscape—along with attention to craftsmanship and detail. Two-story houses and one- or one-and-a-half-story bungalows typically have low roofs and wide eave overhangs, as well as projecting gabled dormers with decorative brackets and sometimes balconies.

Under low sloping roofs, the broad front entry porches are deep and dark, providing shade from the southern California sun. In a way similar to that in Prairie-style porches, roofs are supported by tapered columns on thick masonry piers and sided with clapboard or wood shingles that are naturally weathered or stained a dark, rich brown. Bungalow doors often have simple geometric designs, not unlike those found in Prairie-style entrances: small squares or tall and narrow panes of glass set side by side, with the pattern repeated in the windows.

The Bandini bungalow, built in 1903 in Pasadena, California, and the Charles M. Pratt house, built in 1909 in Ojai, California, are well-known examples of both the Arts and Crafts movement in this country and Greene & Greene design. Smaller, simpler, and more modest versions of the Craftsman bungalow were built from coast to coast after house plans for it appeared in *The Craftsman* and *American Bungalow* magazines, and Sears, Roebuck began offering mail-order models with precut lumber. It was also one of the earliest examples of the middle-class American model house, built by contractor-builders in large numbers and in a great variety of substyles.

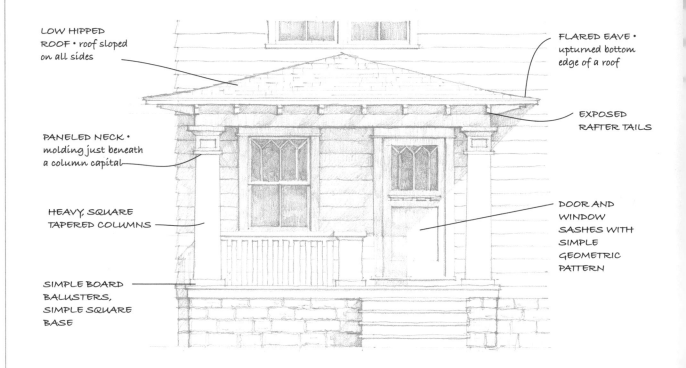

LOW HIPPED
ROOF • roof sloped
on all sides

FLARED EAVE •
upturned bottom
edge of a roof

EXPOSED
RAFTER TAILS

PANELED NECK •
molding just beneath
a column capital

HEAVY, SQUARE
TAPERED COLUMNS

DOOR AND
WINDOW
SASHES WITH
SIMPLE
GEOMETRIC
PATTERN

SIMPLE BOARD
BALUSTERS,
SIMPLE SQUARE
BASE

Craftsman/Bungalow Entrance

Inspired by the Arts and Crafts movement in England, Craftsman bungalows combined attention to craftsmanship and details with American simplicity and efficiency. Natural materials, such as native stone piers and Douglas fir siding, gave the houses a rusticated look, though with flair: The piers and shortened columns are tapered, and the shingles varied and staggered.

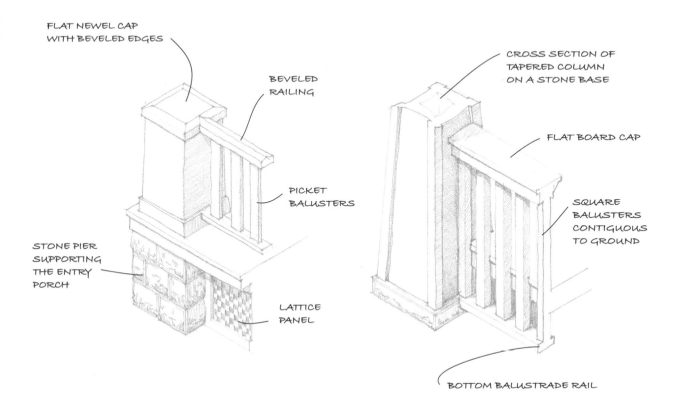

FLAT NEWEL CAP
WITH BEVELED EDGES

BEVELED
RAILING

CROSS SECTION OF
TAPERED COLUMN
ON A STONE BASE

FLAT BOARD CAP

PICKET
BALUSTERS

SQUARE
BALUSTERS
CONTIGUOUS
TO GROUND

STONE PIER
SUPPORTING
THE ENTRY
PORCH

LATTICE
PANEL

BOTTOM BALUSTRADE RAIL

Craftsman/Bungalow Balustrades

Balustrades were typically straightforward constructions on bungalow porches. Their very
simplicity made them both appealing and affordable to a broad segment of the population.
In the left-hand drawing, the beveled railing caps board-picket balusters. On the right, the
flat railing holds square sticks. Bottom rails anchor both balusters to the flooring.

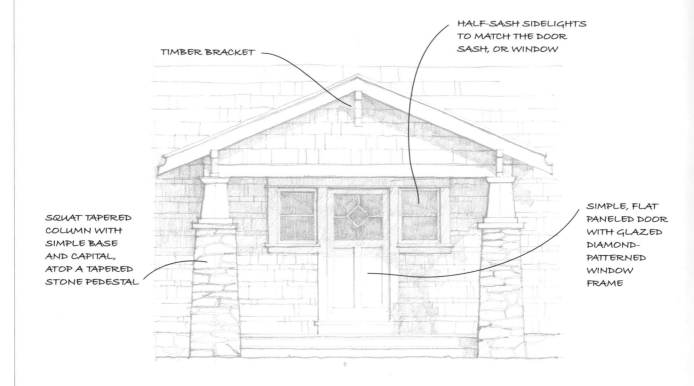

TIMBER BRACKET

HALF-SASH SIDELIGHTS TO MATCH THE DOOR SASH, OR WINDOW

SQUAT TAPERED COLUMN WITH SIMPLE BASE AND CAPITAL, ATOP A TAPERED STONE PEDESTAL

SIMPLE, FLAT PANELED DOOR WITH GLAZED DIAMOND-PATTERNED WINDOW FRAME

Craftsman/Bungalow Gabled Porch

Neither grand nor crude, the standard Craftsman bungalow entry porch had enough room and grace for the average American. Between 1910 and 1940, the bungalow was one of the most popular house styles in the country. Emphasizing its commonality, as well as the integrity of the form, the foundation is of plain cut stone, the balusters of straight stock, and the rafter tails in the porch's hipped roof exposed. Half-sash sidelights match the glazed section of the front door.

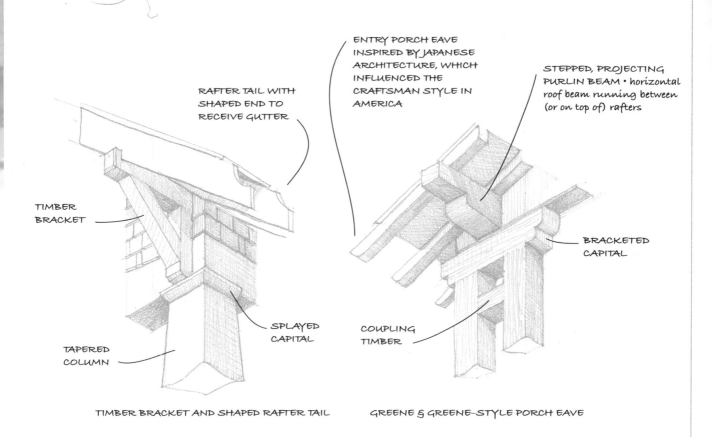

RAFTER TAIL WITH
SHAPED END TO
RECEIVE GUTTER

ENTRY PORCH EAVE
INSPIRED BY JAPANESE
ARCHITECTURE, WHICH
INFLUENCED THE
CRAFTSMAN STYLE IN
AMERICA

STEPPED, PROJECTING
PURLIN BEAM · horizontal
roof beam running between
(or on top of) rafters

TIMBER
BRACKET

BRACKETED
CAPITAL

TAPERED
COLUMN

SPLAYED
CAPITAL

COUPLING
TIMBER

TIMBER BRACKET AND SHAPED RAFTER TAIL

GREENE & GREENE-STYLE PORCH EAVE

Craftsman/Bungalow Brackets and Columns

Most bungalow columns and brackets were plain and inexpensive, but there was freedom
to add fine details and elaborations. The rafter tails in the drawing on the left have shaped
ends to receive the gutter, and the tapered porch column has a splayed capital. The porch
eave on the right is representative of high-style Craftsman bungalows; Greene & Greene
borrowed this elaborate post-and-bracket composition from traditional Japanese pavilion
design.

MODERN PERIOD

1920 – 1940

ART DECO STYLE
1925 – 1930

Art Deco describes the modernist movement and style that became fashionable in the 1920s and 1930s. The term came into vogue following the Exposition Internationale des Arts Décoratifs and Industriels Modernes in Paris in 1925 and grew to extend far beyond architecture to eventually include paintings, jewelry, trains, cruise ships, cars, furniture, and home appliances.

In rejecting historical revivalist traditions and embracing modern architectural and artistic concepts, Art Deco structures tend to be vertical, streamlined, and futuristic, with geometrical design patterns—chevrons, zigzags, lightning bolts, and abstract shells and sunrises—that, ironically, were influenced by the Arts and Crafts movement and by pre-Columbian and Native American arts. Concrete and stucco, steel, chrome, brushed aluminum, and glass, the materials used in the construction of these sleek twentieth-century facades were bold and daring for the times.

Many more skyscrapers and office buildings than private residences were built in this style, predominantly in New York City. William Van Allen's 1930 design of the Chrysler Building represents the pinnacle of Art Deco commercial architecture. Its needle-nosed spire, manufactured from nickel chromium, is 180 feet high. The radiating zigzag design is a visual reference to the crown on the Statue of Liberty.

On the West Coast, Art Deco found expression in theaters (Grauman's Chinese Theatre on Hollywood Boulevard is a good example) as well as in apartment buildings and private residences. Frank Lloyd Wright designed several Art Deco houses, including the John Storer House in Los Angeles in 1923. In Miami, Florida, one section of the city is full of Art Deco apartment buildings and houses and is, obviously, called the Art Deco District.

Art Deco houses were considered eccentric at the time, and little wonder. The verticality that marks commercial Art Deco design is replicated in residential windows and entrances, which were decorated with a melange of new and strange materials: sculpted metalwork, colored marble, and glass bricks. The doors themselves were usually narrow, simple compositions of horizontal glass panes and wood or aluminum, but they might have semicircular canopies or be capped with upward-thrusting projections, short towers, or stepped hoods.

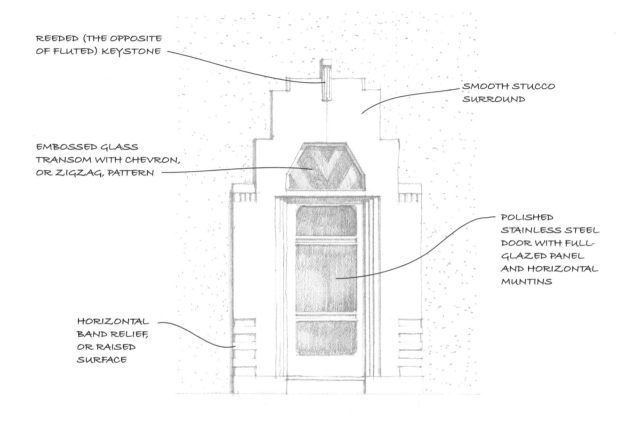

REEDED (THE OPPOSITE OF FLUTED) KEYSTONE

SMOOTH STUCCO SURROUND

EMBOSSED GLASS TRANSOM WITH CHEVRON, OR ZIGZAG, PATTERN

POLISHED STAINLESS STEEL DOOR WITH FULL-GLAZED PANEL AND HORIZONTAL MUNTINS

HORIZONTAL BAND RELIEF, OR RAISED SURFACE

Art Deco Entrance

The doorway in this drawing might easily be mistaken for a cigarette lighter from the 1930s. Following the Exposition Internationale des Arts Décoratifs and Industriels Modernes in Paris in 1925, in fact, Art Deco design spread to many areas of modern life. In architecture, the futuristic thrust of Art Deco theaters, corporate buildings, and private residences gave rise to sleek entrances of concrete and stainless steel that looked as if they were ready for liftoff. Door surrounds included chevrons and other geometrical designs abstracted from nature.

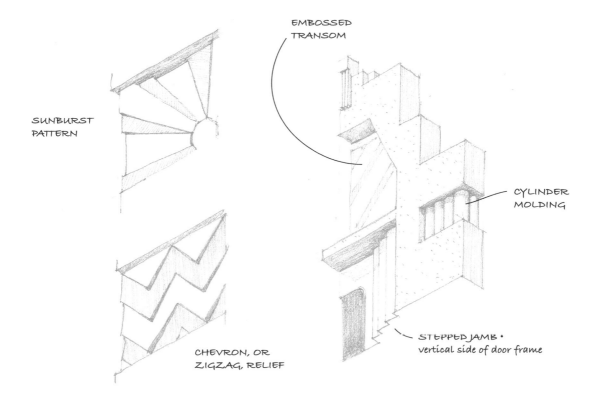

SUNBURST
PATTERN

EMBOSSED
TRANSOM

CYLINDER
MOLDING

CHEVRON, OR
ZIGZAG, RELIEF

STEPPED JAMB •
vertical side of door frame

Art Deco Bas-relief Designs

Art Deco entrances employed a number of devices to achieve an early-space-age (via Flash Gordon) effect, including concrete steps and bas-relief. Art Deco design patterns—chevrons, zigzags, lightning bolts, and abstract shells and sunrises—were inspired in part by Cubism.

MODERNIST STYLE
1920 – 1940

"Modern" is a broad, all-inclusive term for a collection of twentieth-century styles and the architects associated with them: Frank Lloyd Wright, Walter Gropius, Mies van der Rohe, and Le Corbusier. They and others held that form should follow function, making ornamentation superfluous and the historical revival trends of the past centuries irrelevant. Their concerns were with structural form, new engineering techniques and materials, and abstract notions of beauty.

For our purposes, modern means two particular movements and styles—Modernist (also known as Art Moderne) and Art Deco—that entered the vernacular between the 1920s and 1940s. The house styles that became popular after 1930, and are included in this book, are Ranches, Foursquares, Builders' Colonials, and Capes. These forms, which largely defined, and continue to define, suburban America, are discussed in the next section, where drawings of classic entrances are superimposed on them.

Typical Modernist buildings are boxes of stucco, concrete over steel, or vertical flush-board siding with gently curved corners, flat roofs, horizontal bands of plate or glass-block windows, and sometimes second-story decks with horizontal metal railings. The whole emphasis, in fact (unlike Art Deco design), is on low horizontal lines, following the notion that the form and structure of the building, rather than historical references, are the "decoration."

Lacking ornamentation or emphasis, Modernist entranceways are often recessed or tucked under a simple concrete overhang. The doors themselves might contain horizontal glass panes but are otherwise unadorned, favoring instead a cleanness and simplicity of line that is starkly appealing. Radio City Music Hall at Rockefeller Center in New York City is a commercial example of the style. The Butler House in Des Moines, Iowa, designed in 1917, is a model Modernist house.

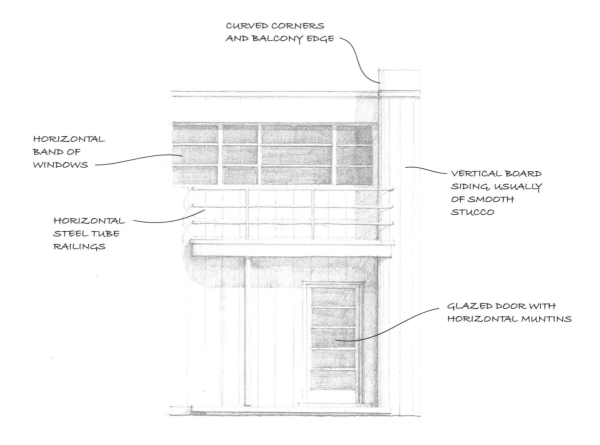

CURVED CORNERS
AND BALCONY EDGE

HORIZONTAL
BAND OF
WINDOWS

HORIZONTAL
STEEL TUBE
RAILINGS

VERTICAL BOARD
SIDING, USUALLY
OF SMOOTH
STUCCO

GLAZED DOOR WITH
HORIZONTAL MUNTINS

Modernist Entrance

Inasmuch as "modern architecture" is a term subject to interpretation and continual change, there may be no representative modern entrance. But the collection of early-twentieth-century modern styles called Modernist shares characteristics with later examples. Buildings were boxes with horizontal lines and smooth cladding of concrete, stucco, stainless steel, and glass. Entrances followed suit—as in this drawing of a glass door with horizontal divides—maintaining low, unornamented profiles in the pursuit of the modern edict that form follows function. This is the way in, nothing more and nothing less.

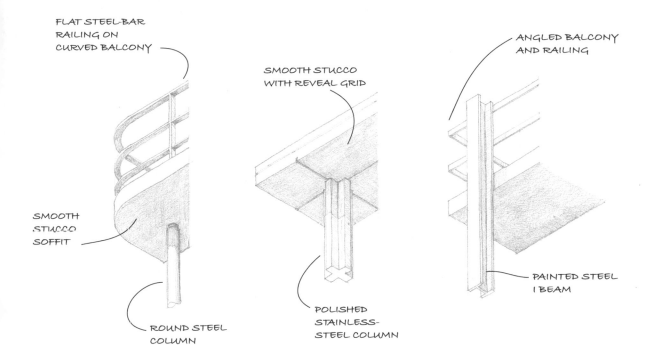

FLAT STEEL-BAR
RAILING ON
CURVED BALCONY

SMOOTH STUCCO
WITH REVEAL GRID

ANGLED BALCONY
AND RAILING

SMOOTH
STUCCO
SOFFIT

ROUND STEEL
COLUMN

POLISHED
STAINLESS-
STEEL COLUMN

PAINTED STEEL
I BEAM

Modernist Balconies and Columns

The early-twentieth-century architecture called Modernist favored sleek balconies, frequently over doorways, that reiterated the minimalism of the buildings themselves: slick, strong materials—smooth concrete and stucco, polished stainless steel and steel beams—and clean lines that served as the only ornamentation.

Part Two

ADAPTATIONS

INTRODUCTION

Evolving over the course of thousands of years, classic entrances have endured for a number of reasons. They are equally practical and beautiful. They signify the importance of a house and its place in the community and immediately identify its style and owners' taste. Some types shelter guests from the elements and serve as transitional spaces between the exterior and the interior. Others are so well designed that they direct, simply but powerfully, all attention to the center of the house. Each represents a period of history and style. Each introduces the house to the world.

For this section of the book, we chose a number of classic entrances and imagined how they might look if adapted for standard, present-day suburban houses. We then added these adaptations to the facades of four basic styles: Ranches, Foursquares, Builders' Colonials, and Capes.

Which entrance styles work with which houses? Consulting an architect can best answer that question. Beyond being able to recommend appropriate matches, professionals can determine the right entrance size, roof pitch (if there is an overhang or portico), and mix of elements and details, such as windows, molding, ornaments, stonework, and hardware. But as most architects and builders will tell you, the more clearly home owners are able to envision and articulate what they want, the easier it is to come up with a satisfying design. Discovering what matches you like in this section should greatly help you with the design process.

Many of the entrances we've selected fit naturally by virtue of belonging to the same architectural family as the houses to which they've been adapted. Builders' Colonials, for example, evolved from Georgians and Federals, which in turn evolved from early-Colonial-period houses. Some entrances and houses have form and scale in common. The Cape's boxlike simplicity and modest proportions make it ideal for Craftsman/Bungalow entrances and also for Colonial Revival, Greek Revival, and, surprisingly, Gothic Revival entrances. Ranches, meanwhile, share certain traits—low roofs and profiles, horizontal floor plans—with Prairie and Craftsman houses, yet leave room for conversions to everything from Classical to Art Deco and Modernist entrances.

Often, adding a classic entrance entails a little more than fitting a new door and molding, and maybe a transom or pair of flanking sidelights. Where a classical portico is called for or suggested, the portico roof will have to be tied into the frame of the house and often a wood or stone base constructed for supporting the columns. In the most adventurous or imaginative remodels, of course, the exterior walls, windows, and roof must adapt to the new look.

Fortunately, today a wide range of entrance details—from antique architectural artifacts to period reproductions—can be found in salvage yards, lumber stores, or online catalogs. Other resources can be easily located in the back of home remodeling magazines, whose legions have grown in leaps and bounds in recent years. What isn't available from those sources can be custom-made by carpenters or woodworking mills.

Yet any style you choose from this section, or any combination of elements you come up with on your own, is likely to have a significant impact on your house. Even the most minor of entrance adaptations will change the house's character, feeling, appearance, and curb appeal. And, in the process and seemingly overnight, your house will be transformed from a one-of-many to a one-of-a-kind home.

RANCHES

Ranches (or Ramblers, as they're referred to in the Midwest) grew out of a number of distinctly different house styles: Japanese, California Bungalow, and Prairie. After World War II, affordable housing developments began cropping up farther from cities, allowing for larger lots and more horizontal house plans. Then, as now, they were one-story buildings with low hipped or side-gabled roofs with wide front eaves. Entrances were hidden or minimized under the roof overhangs, especially once built-in garages became part of the package and the primary portal to the home. For the earliest Ranch owners, the style represented an escape from the past and an advance toward modernism and the American dream. Whatever the reasons for their appeal, "Ranchburgers" (as they've disparagingly been called) dominated the suburbs in the 1950s and 1960s, spreading out across America as if there were no end to the landscape, and no tomorrow. The low linearity of Ranches almost invites renovation and permits a wide range of entrance possibilities.

Classical Revival Ranch

The nondescript nature of most Ranches helps when adapting a classic entrance. This basic suburban house can become practically any other architectural style, even Classical Revival (in a way, the antithesis of twentieth-century suburbia), by means of a few changes. It's possible to do the minimal by installing a new paneled front door, then tacking on shutters and a small pediment. Here, though, the classical style is fully expressed in the addition of a cross gable, cut into the existing, low-pitched roof, to create a prominent, central portico. To match the cross gable, the eaves of the old roof are extended with thick trimwork and inset with lunettes, or half-round windows. The entablature is also carried around the exterior. Is all this extra woodwork necessary? Maybe not, but it helps tie the new addition to the old house. What is necessary—at least to affect the classical look—is the use of flanking pairs of Doric columns to support the portico from a raised stoop. Wood columns feel more substantial to the touch, but new architectural columns made of fiberglass, which cost about ten percent more, look as good and last much longer.

And while brick veneer is right for this adaptation, clapboard, which is much less expensive, can also be used to achieve a similar look. In general, the trick with this adaptation lies in proportion and scale, and therefore in the hands of an architect or competent builder: The portico should be big enough to alter the character of the structure, but not so big as to overwhelm the rest of the house.

California Craftsman/Bungalow Ranch

A little more imagination may be needed to visualize a Craftsman/Bungalow Ranch, and perhaps more effort to adapt this style of entrance. But again, the linearity of typical Ranch houses suits conversion to Craftsman bungalows, with their offset entrances. And the opportunity to turn a low, stark rectangle of space into a cozy-looking cottage seems hard to resist. As in the other treatments in this section, the big cross gable opens up part of the interior ceiling and doubles as a handsome entry porch, here with extended exposed rafters and squat Craftsman-style piers and columns. The new gable and roof overhangs can be built over the existing roof; wood shingles, the appropriate cladding for the style, can replace the existing siding. Reproductions of period Craftsman doors, which usually feature geometric patterns in the glass, can be found online. So can the tapered porch posts and rafter brackets, although experienced carpenters can also make these items on-site. The piers under the posts are generally stone, but they can also be built of brick, stucco, or wood.

Prairie Ranch

Ranches evolved in part from Prairie houses, and perhaps more than any other possible matching, the Ranch plays into the horizontality of the earlier style. Few adaptations work so well. At the same time, though, adapting an early-twentieth century Prairie-style entrance to a 1950s-style Ranch means, at least in our rendering, turning the latter into a Frank Lloyd Wright–like house, which requires a total renovation of the existing exterior. The major renovation and additions are to the existing roof and new entry roof projection. Beyond changing the roof from side-gabled to hipped, which would transform the interior as well as the facade of the house, the roof eaves are extended out as far as possible in order to realize fully the ambitions of the preceding style. If the front door is changed to the period style (like other architectural elements, Prairie reproductions are readily available from catalogs and online), the old sash windows should be replaced with wide bands of Wright-like windows, and not just across the front but on all sides of the house. Widening and flattening the chimney stack, which Wright used to contrast the flatness of the roof, is another element that could be copied.

FOURSQUARES

Between 1890 and 1930, the Foursquare was the Everyman of American houses—a simple, practical, nearly square-shaped box designed for small city lots. (A smaller version, the one-story Workingman's Foursquare, was developed in quantity by companies for their employees around World War I.) Models varied in style and materials, some borrowing features from the Prairie and Craftsman styles. The standard Foursquare, however, was two and a half stories, with a pyramidal hipped roof and matching front dormer. It had a front porch with a wide stoop and centered paneled door; brick, stucco, concrete block, or wood siding; and minimal decoration. The floor plan resembled that of a bungalow, with four rooms of nearly equal size both upstairs and downstairs. Simplicity and affordability (prices ranged from $2,000 to $5,000) made the style popular as a kit home. Montgomery Ward and Sears, Roebuck offered dozens of models, including kits with numbered parts shipped by rail. Foursquares, found in urban and older suburban neighborhoods across the country, readily lend themselves to classic entrance conversions that simply aren't possible in other houses.

Craftsman/Bungalow Foursquare

The standard Foursquare stands taller than the average Craftsman house or Craftsman bungalow, but the houses share similar shapes, roofs, and porch styles. Actually, the full-width entry porch shown here is a sort of hybrid Craftsman/Prairie style: low hipped roof with wide overhang; rafters that are extended, exposed, and tapered; thick columns with minimal detailing; and simple stick balusters. While the porch fits the squat Foursquare form, it also breaks up the mass of the house, softens the severe outer edge of the facade, and gives the house both the extra dimension and a casual comfort zone it lacked. As is true of most of the houses in this book, details count almost as much as structural change. A small detail here is the use of wood shingles, which are warmer and closer to the bungalow tradition than the stone facing or aluminum siding frequently found on Foursquares. The big details are the windows and front door, which feature vertical diamond glazing of the type found in high-style Prairie homes. Replacing the windows around the house would probably exceed the cost of building the porch, but the charm factor is immediate and significant.

Mediterranean Foursquare

An adaptation as extensive as the one shown here requires considerable effort and money, yet the resulting shift in architectural climates—from Brooklyn or Chicago in the 1940s to Hollywood or Palm Beach in the 1920s, all without leaving the old neighborhood—may well be worth it. This makeover also illustrates the adaptability of the Foursquare. Since the existing hipped roof is common to Mediterranean houses, it stays in the picture; but because the Mediterranean style is so distinctive, everything else on the exterior needs to change: red terra-cotta tiles (or red asphalt roof shingles), ornamental eave brackets, metal- or wood-framed casement windows, and stuccoed walls. Meanwhile, the entrance is a small work of European art. The arched and paneled door, characteristic of early Mediterranean mansions, might be found in architectural salvage yards or a reproduction bought new online; otherwise, it has to be custom-made. The door is recessed in a surround of limestone blocks, which can be simulated in colored stucco or wood and hooded with a second-story wrought-iron balcony. When all is said and, especially, done, the house is still a Foursquare—it's just less stark, and much warmer and more exotic, than it used to be.

Second Empire Foursquare

It may sound somewhat surprising that so basic an American house could adopt the stately architectural style of late-nineteenth-century France. Essentially, both are simple boxes, however, with similar masses if dissimilar ambitions. This loose and modest interpretation of a Second Empire mansion is more democratic than Napoleonic; it lacks the tower, cupola, iron crestings, balconies, or thick moldings from that period (see pages 72–75). Still, the effect of combining the two styles is atmospheric and romantic. The most distinguishing characteristic of the earlier style is the mansard roof. Even though it can be built over the existing Foursquare roof, it's a big change, and a sizeable production and expense. But the shape and extra height permit a third-story curved-roofed dormer (another Second Empire characteristic and another expense!). More impressive and resonant is the single-story entrance porch. Sweeping Renaissance-inspired arches, which rest on handsome tapered posts, frame the entrance and fully balance the squareness of the house. To accommodate the double front doors and curved transom, the original doorway has to be widened and reframed. The ideal new home owner for this type of adaptation will probably have to love Second Empire houses, yet not necessarily be in the market for an original.

BUILDERS' COLONIALS

Like Capes and Ranches, Colonials are among the most ubiquitous of American houses. Although the first New England Colonials had a late-medieval mass and a puritanical spareness, they evolved to larger and more varied styles: Dutch, French, and Spanish Colonials; Georgian and Adam Colonials; and Early Classical Revival Colonials. In the latter half of the twentieth century, Builders' Colonials swept the continent, filling in the suburban landscape. Economical to build, relatively inexpensive to buy, and familiar to live in, they bear a remarkable resemblance to the earliest examples of the style: two-story rectangles with a gabled roof, central front door frequently flush with the facade, and little ornamentation. Their proportions and plainness make Builders' Colonials perfect candidates for a wide range of classic entrances.

Georgian Colonial

At the end of the nineteenth century, when Georgians began replacing pre-Revolutionary Colonials as the most fashionable American house style, they did so with doorways, moldings, and ornamental woodwork. Since then, the Colonial form hasn't really changed; it's basically a two-story rectangle that can be upgraded by virtue of the same elements. "Georgian Colonial doorways" are more than a pair of narrow, paneled, double doors— a handsome feature of the period style. They are entrance compositions, from which the doors are inseparable. However, there are degrees of elaboration or detailing based on taste, adherence to historical correctness, and budget. In this drawing, we set the doors in a paneled recess, surrounded the doorway with Corinthian pilasters on paneled bases, and capped it with a thick frieze (the usually decorative horizontal band spanning an entrance) and a broken pediment that showcases a carved wooden pineapple (the "welcome" symbol in the New England colonies; reproductions of this and other architectural artifacts are easy to find). The replacement window over the doorway is tied into the composition. But we could have created a simpler entrance using plain pilasters, fewer moldings, and a broken or solid pediment without ornament. In either event, with no structural change, a cookie-cutter Builders' Colonial can become a formal, even grand, house. Although the roofs could be hipped and the windows capped with low pediments, as they often were in nineteenth-century Georgian houses, here they're not. Also optional are details such as the egg-and-dart molding across the top of the front wall, frieze and decorative corbels under the eaves, and quoins, or cut-stone blocks (or wood simulating stone), up the corners of the house.

Federal Colonial

A still more refined doorway is possible when adapting the Federal (or Adam) style to a standard twentieth- or twenty-first-century Colonial. Evolving from Georgian houses, Federal doorways usually incorporated curves and ellipses, often in the form of fanlight windows. The new/old door and fanlight shown here might suffice, bringing soft lines and grace to the Colonial's flat facade and sharp angles. But for a house this size—and a Federal adaptation at its grandest—we added a formal portico, plinth or stoop, and balcony. All are rounded in the Federal style, following the curve of the doorway. The classical columns, in concert with the fluted pilasters, are tapered and more slender than those typically found on Georgian entrances. The second-story balustrade serves as the crown of the enterprise and is for effect rather than public announcements (as was occasionally the case during the Federal period in England). We also added some optional elements: quarter-round windows in the gable eaves on either side of the chimney, which echo the lines of the portico; and the freizeboard above the second-floor windows, expressing a Federal pattern of interlocking ropes. The result of all this change is an entrance that shelters arriving guests, provides a stylish transition space between the outdoors and indoors, and calls attention to itself and the house in an elegant way.

Italianate Colonial

One of the pleasures of architecture is imagining the possibilities for everyday houses—for example, this Italianate entry porch, doorway, and facade for a contemporary suburban Colonial. Inspired by farmhouses found in Colonial America and the Italian countryside, nineteenth-century Italianate houses frequently had hipped roofs, but some were cross gabled (meaning the inverted V-shaped ends of a double-sloped roof are perpendicular to each other), like the model on the opposite page. For this adaptation to work, there's no getting around the inclusion of the big, central cross gable, which involves cutting into the main roof, then framing, sheathing, and shingling the new gable. What the cross gable does is give the house the height needed to fully adapt the new style and to incorporate two signature Italianate characteristics: the wide overhang on the new roof and the ornate brackets beneath the overhang. Of course, it also opens up the third story of the house and creates the opportunity for another Italianate touch—the small, rounded attic window with U-shaped hood. Both the gable and the new window help pull the eye to the entrance. Although the double front doorway is rounded, too, the entry porch with low hipped roof also references the Italianate style and heightens the experience of arriving and departing. The porch arcade is composed of paired posts that are beveled, set on paneled pedestals, and echoed in pairings of porch overhang brackets. The one option here may be the old-fashioned large-paned windows in place of the standard-issue, six-over-six windows on the facade, but it's hard to imagine the adaptation without them.

CAPE CODS

In the late 1600s, New World settlers began building small, compact houses up and down Cape Cod and other coastal and riverine parts of Massachusetts and Connecticut. These early examples were reminiscent of Dutch and English cottages, particularly those found in Devon and Cornwall in the west of England, with flush, unsheltered, and unornamented doorways. Yet, at the same time, they possessed a style of their own: They were a story or story and a half high, frequently with a central entrance, an eight-to-twelve-pitch roof, and, as the form evolved, symmetrical dormers in front and frequently a shed dormer in back. By the mid-1940s and the end of World War II, returning GIs found center-hall Capes desirable and affordable. They were America's first "starter" houses.

Colonial Cape

English Colonials belong to the same family of early New England houses as Capes, so that elements from one work well on the other. Although the standard Colonial is two stories high, rather than one or one and a half stories, and larger and more rectangular than the Cape, the two styles share end-gabled roofs, central doorways, and symmetrical placement of windows across the front of the house. The simplest and least expensive change to make is the addition of sidelights on either side of the front door. This not only "Colonializes" a typical Cape, it brings daylight into the house and casts welcoming, interior light onto the front stoop. An added portico, as shown in this drawing, further transforms the house, referencing the evolution of New England houses and aligning it with Federal- (or Adam-) style Colonials. The portico also creates a covered entrance, extending the usable space of the smaller Cape. Note that the new gabled roof has the same pitch (the slope of the roof) as the existing main roof and dormers, and the entrance's height and projection are in scale with the house as a whole. The detailing here is simple, too, in keeping with a Cape's typically modest profile. Another inexpensive touch is the built-in benches, found in early Dutch Colonials. They partially enclose the portico, beckon visitors, and turn the entranceway into an inviting anteroom.

Greek Revival Cape

In their shape and mass (the visual weight of a house), most Capes resemble the basic temple form, making them likely candidates for revival through the addition of a one-story, classical Greek doorway. Like their ancient Mediterranean counterparts, perhaps, the first Capes were built by fishermen settling the Massachusetts coast; and by the nineteenth century and the boom in the American import-export trade, it was sea captains who commissioned some of the grandest Greek Revival mansions on the New England coast. The adapted entry shown here is a classical composition of outer pilasters, flanking sidelights, and inner Ionic columns—all under a shallow pediment. (On most Capes, there is room between the top of the windows and the eaves for a classical entablature, but only enough room for a low pediment such as this.) While it may look elaborate, this entrance is a minor adaptation. Any good carpenter could construct it using materials ordered from a high-end lumber yard or online catalog of architectural woodwork, plus a set of plans, either from a pattern book or an architect. The Greek temple effect can be extended across the entire front of the house by means of two additional architectural items: a facia (or flat, horizontal board over an opening) with molding running the width of the facade and corner pilasters at either end of the house. This adaptation ennobles an otherwise humble house and allows it to stand out—by virtue of class and style, rather than a huge addition, in developments of nearly replicate structures.

Gothic Revival Cape

As popularized by Andrew Jackson Downing in books such as *Cottage Residences,* the Gothic Revival cottage is similar in size and spirit to basic Capes, especially those with steep-pitched roofs. Highly characteristic of the Gothic Revival style, and the first and easiest place to start in an adaptation of this kind, is the lance-arched door and casing. Since the doorway shown here is flattened against the facade (as are standard Cape entries), however, we also added a three-quarter-length entrance porch—a not-uncommon feature in the mid-nineteenth century. The porch, which is a fairly uncomplicated addition, creates an outdoor room while setting the stage for the new doorway. The fascia boards and porch railings feature scroll-saw ornamentation that is typical of the original style. Pieces like this can be easily made up by woodworking mills or skilled carpenters. Although not essential, to complete the transformation, we added high two-over-two (two panes over two panes) windows on the first level, and dressed up the dormers with vergeboards (gable trim work) and pinnacles. Rather than updating the Cape, a Gothic Revival adaptation rusticates it and turns a standard house into an exotic-looking cottage with considerable appeal and mystique.

GLOSSARY

Italicized words in the definitions are also included in this glossary.

 ABACUS the uppermost element of a column's *capital (37)*

ACROTERIUM a pedestal or ornament at a *pediment*'s ends *(57)*

ANNULATED COLUMN a post shaped at intervals with circles or rings *(83)*

ARCADE a line of arches, often along a covered walk, on piers or columns *(74)*

ARCH a curved span over an entrance *(114)*

ARCHITRAVE in classical architecture, the lower part of the *entablature,* or the section between a column *capital* and roof or *pediment (44)*

ASTRAGAL a half-round molding often decorated with beads

ATTIC BASE the base of an *Ionic column (43)*

BALL FINIAL a ball-shaped ornament terminating the top of a post or other vertical element *(42)*

BALUSTER the upright stick of a *balustrade* railing *(125)*

BALUSTRADE a railing enclosing a balcony, widow's walk, etc. *(32)*

BAND COURSE a horizontal, often projecting, member marking a division in a wall surface *(111)*

BAND WINDOWS a broad series of same-size windows set close together *(120)*

BARGEBOARD a wide board used to trim the edges of a *gable* (also called *vergeboard*) *(82, 61)*

 BAS-RELIEF a shallow carved or embossed figure or design protruding from a wall or other flat surface *(45)*

BATTEN DOOR an unframed wooden door of usually rough, vertical boards fastened to horizontal or Z-shaped battens (narrow horizontal strips of wood) on the inside *(107)*

BATTLEMENT a *parapet,* usually found on fortified castle walls, with alternating open and solid sections *(62)*

BED MOLDING the bottom element of a group of moldings, or any molding beneath a projection *(37)*

BELT COURSE (or *stringcourse*) a belt of horizontal boards, shingles, bricks, etc., around a house *(78)*

BEVEL an angled edge *(125)*

BOARD AND BATTEN adjacent vertical planks with joints concealed by wood strips *(62, 107)*

BOLECTION MOLDING ornamental molding concealing the joint between surfaces that are on different levels *(36)*

BRACKET a projecting member, often ornamental, supporting an entrance roof or overhang *(69)*

BROKEN PEDIMENT a *pediment* (over a doorway) that's interrupted in the center by ornamental woodwork such as a pineapple, urn, or cartouche *(35)*

CAPITAL the uppermost element of a column or *pilaster (56)*

CASEMENT a window that swings out on side hinges *(62, 114)*

CASING the exterior trim or framing around a door or window *(67, 105)*

CASTELLATED castlelike *(62)*

CHAMFER a *bevel* or slant; an angled edge *(60)*

CHEEK WALL a low, upright face of wall, especially one framing an opening and projecting beyond the envelope of a building *(57)*

CHEVRON an ornamental, V-shaped design first used in Romanesque architecture and most commonly associated with Art Deco *(133)*

CLADDING any exterior wall sheathing or covering

CLAPBOARD tapered wood strips, overlapped and usually of cedar, used to side a house *(49)*

CLASSICAL ARCHITECTURE the building style of ancient Greece and Rome *(48, 49)*

COLLAR BEAM a horizontal member connecting opposite rafters *(61)*

COLLAR BRACE a member supporting a *collar beam (104)*

COLONNADE a series of columns arranged in ordered intervals *(48, 49)*

COPING a cap of wood, stone, or metal *(111)*

CORBEL a supporting bracket or projecting block *(30)*

CORINTHIAN COLUMN a slender, fluted Grecian or Roman column with ornate, leaflike carvings around the *capital (42)*

CORNICE the projected molding that finishes a *hood, pediment, portico,* etc.; also the uppermost section of a classic *entablature (44)*

COUPLING TIMBER a horizontal member connecting pillars or posts *(88, 127)*

COVE concave; usually concave molding *(69)*

COVED BRACKET a concave *bracket (69, 79)*

CRENELLATED MOLDING molding notched to represent the top of a fortified wall *(62)*

CRESTING an ornamental roof projection *(75)*

CROSS GABLES *gables* set perpendicular to one another

CROWN the uppermost part, whether structural or ornamental, of a window, door, or other architectural element *(36)*

CUSHION CAPITAL a stone or wood *capital* resembling a flattened cushion with the bottom edges rounded *(95)*

DADO the middle section of a *pedestal (37)*

DENTIL MOLDING toothlike ornamental molding typically found above exterior doorways and under *eaves (31, 45, 74)*

DIAPER a pattern repeated across horizontal and diagonal grids *(96)*

DORIC COLUMN a thick, often fluted classical column with simple, saucer-shaped *capital (56)*

DORMER a small attic or upper-floor window set vertically in the roof

DOVECOTE a series of square nesting niches for pigeons *(94)*

DUTCH DOOR a door divided into upper and lower halves that swing independently of each other *(23)*

EAR a small projecting member, usually on door or window *casings (35, 67)*

EASTLAKE DESIGN a decorative design in the style of British designer Charles Eastlake, marked by rich ornamentation *(75)*

EAVE an overhang at the bottom edge of a roof *(88, 120)*

ECHINUS the curved projecting molding supporting the *abacus* of a Doric column *(37)*

EGG-AND-DART MOLDING a pattern of repeating oval and arrow shapes *(45)*

ELLIPTICAL FANLIGHT a window shaped like an ellipse or wide, horizontal oval, placed over a door *(31, 41)*

ENGAGED COLUMN a column built into a wall *(31)*

ENTABLATURE in classical architecture, the section of a doorway surround between a column *capital* and *pediment, portico,* or roof edge *(44)*

ENTASIS the convex curving of a tapered column *(56)*

EYEBROW a half-round window or *dormer,* sloped at both ends and usually set into the lower section of a roof

FACADE the front, or face, of a building *(88)*

FALSE PARAPET an ornamental element having the appearance of a low wall at the edge of a roof *(66)*

FANLIGHT a transom window, above an entrance, in the shape of a semicircle or fan with spokelike *muntins (31)*

FANTAIL a decorative panel resembling a fan *(82)*

FASCIA any flat wood member below an *eave (48)*

FESTOON a carved decorative banner or wreath emulating fabric or flowers, often bound with sculpted ribbons *(41)*

FILLET a short, thin strip of rectangular molding *(75, 121)*

FINIAL an ornament at the top of a post, *gable,* etc. *(44)*

FLEUR-DE-LIS a design based on the French royal lily *(115)*

FLUTING the shallow, vertical channels in a column or *pilaster (41, 33)*

FRETWORK ornamental, interlocking design patterns inscribed in relief *(54, 57)*

FRIEZE a decorative horizontal band spanning an entrance or opening *(44)*

GABLE the inverted-V-shaped end of a double-sloped roof *(75, 102)*

GAMBREL a ridged roof with two slopes on either side

GINGERBREAD (also called spindle work) highly decorative woodwork found on American Victorian houses *(83)*

GLAZING the glass used in a house's design *(66)*

GOTHIC ARCH a pointed arch *(60)*

GUTTA a cone-shaped *pendant* *(73)*

 HALF ROUND semicircular window, frequently set in *eaves* *(40, 42, 43)*

HALF-TIMBERING a timber-framed facade where the spaces between frame members are filled with brick, stone, stucco, or all three *(102, 104)*

HIPPED ROOF a four-sloped roof *(124, 148)*

HOOD a cover over a door or window, usually supported by *brackets* *(34)*

INTERLACE a design of entwined, ornamental bands *(45)*

IONIC CAPITAL a capital distinguished by flanking *volutes* *(42, 43)*

IONIC COLUMN a simple, slender Greek column with *volutes* on either side of the *capital* *(49)*

IRIMOYA ROOF a *hipped and gabled roof* found on traditional Japanese buildings *(120)*

JAMB the vertical side of a door frame *(107)*

KEYSTONE the wedge-shaped stone or wood ornament in the top center of an *arch* *(26)*

KING POST the vertical member between the apex of rafter joints and the lower crossbeam or *tie beam* *(78)*

LATTICEWORK an ornamental network of wood strips or laths in straight or diagonal patterns *(62)*

LINTEL the horizontal support, of wood or stone, spanning an opening *(24, 49)*

LOGGIA an open *arcade* or *colonnade* *(94)*

LUNETTE a semicircular window set in an *arch* or *eave* *(48)*

MANSARD ROOF a roof with a double slope on all sides

MASS the visual weight of a building; its overall shape and size *(88)*

MEANDER a labyrinthlike *fretwork* design (also called a Greek key) *(57)*

METOPE in classical architecture, the space between two *triglyphs* *(37)*

 MODILLION decorative *bracket* used to support the *cornice* *(37)*

MULLION the vertical member between units of windows and door panels *(24)*

MUNTIN thin divider between panes of glass *(40, 41, 114)*

NECKING molding beneath a column *capital* *(56)*

NEWEL POSTS the upright posts at the bottom and top of stairs that provide structural stability for the rail *(23, 68)*

 NOGGING brick or stucco filling between framed walls *(102, 104)*

OGEE MOLDING an S-shaped molding *(74)*

OGEE TIMBER BRACKET a heavy, S-shaped *bracket* *(74)*

ORGANIC ARCHITECTURE an early-twentieth-century philosophy advocating harmony between buildings and their environments *(121)*

OVERHANG a roof edge or upper story projecting beyond the lower story *(22)*

OVOLO MOLDING a convex quarter-circular molding *(74)*

PALLADIAN WINDOW a window composition of a high, arched central window flanked by smaller square or rectangular windows *(32)*

PANTILE an S-shaped roof tile, often of clay *(110, 114)*

PARAPET a low masonry wall, often scallop shaped, at the edge of a roof *(110, 111)*

PATERA a round or oval medallion *(42, 45)*

PEDESTAL the base supporting a column *(37, 85)*

PEDIMENT a low *gable,* or triangular overhang crowning an opening *(25)*

PENDANT (also called pendill and drop finial) a decorative piece of *turned* wood suspended from a roof, *bracket,* etc. *(27)*

PENT ROOF a roof with one, usually shallow, slope; also called shed roof *(23)*

PICTURESQUE an aesthetic concept and movement based on natural beauty; an emotional and evocative response to history, architecture, and landscape

PIER the usually thick support for a column, *arch,* or wall *(94)*

 PILASTER a columnlike pier, usually attached to the *facade* and often decorated with shallow grooves, or *fluting (33)*

PINEAPPLE a carved wooden or plaster representation on a post or *broken pediment* signifying welcome *(35)*

PINNACLE POST a decorative shaft descending from the apex of a *gable (61)*

PITCH the slope of a roof

PLINTH a base, usually square *(33, 37)*

PORTICO a small entry porch, often with a *gabled* roof supported by columns or posts *(31)*

 PURLIN a horizontal roof beam running perpendicular to, and below, the rafters *(127)*

QUATREFOIL a pattern of four lobes, or sections of circles, around either a central open area or independent design *(62, 63)*

QUOIN cut-stone blocks, or wood simulating stone, along the edge of a doorway or the corner of a building *(32, 75)*

RAFTER TAIL the end of a rafter (one of the sloping boards supporting a roof) that projects beyond a wall *(78, 114, 127)*

RAKE the angled edge of a *gable, pediment,* or *portico (48)*

RAKE MOLDING the trim along the *rake,* or angled edge, of a *gable, pediment,* or *portico (49)*

RAKE RETURN the horizontal member or molding that runs level to the *rake (31)*

 RECESSED ENTRY a doorway that is set into the front wall of a house, rather than flush with or projecting from it *(55)*

REGLET a flat, narrow projection between grooves *(69)*

RENDERING an elevation (or vertical) drawing showing materials and details

RETURN MOLDING molding that angles off from its main course *(31)*

REVEAL a small gap or groove between two building materials or systems *(137)*

RIDGE the top of a building where the roof slopes meet

ROSETTE a round design or ornament with a floral motif *(35)*

SASH a window frame *(88, 94)*

SCROLLWORK decorative woodwork produced by a scroll saw *(63)*

SHAKE a tapered or wedge-shaped split-wood *shingle,* usually of cedar *(89)*

SHINGLE a length of wood, slate, asphalt, or other material used for siding or roofing a building *(88, 90)*

SIDELIGHT a fixed window, usually narrow and vertical, flanking a door or larger window *(25)*

 SILL APRON trim or boards beneath the sill, or bottom horizontal member, of a window frame *(67)*

SKEW BLOCK a stone that's flat on the bottom and sloped on the top to support a *gable* or *arch;* also called a kneeler or a gable springer *(95)*

SKIRT a border under a window or at the base of a building (also called an apron) *(88)*

SKIRT ROOF a false roof between stories *(88)*

SOFFIT the undersurface of a beam, *arch,* overhang, etc. *(26, 74, 91)*

SPANDREL a triangle spanning two juxtaposed *arches (74, 106)*

SPINDLE WORK decorative sticks of wood turned on a lathe *(82, 83, 84)*

SPLAYED SHINGLE a wood *shingle* set at any angle to other shingles on the same surface *(103)*

STEPPED arranged like a set of steps *(75, 133)*

STILE an upright member of a frame

STRAP HINGE a door hinge with long flaps *(102, 107)*

STRINGCOURSE a horizontal band around the *facade* of a building *(154)*

STYLOBATE a continuous *plinth* on which a row of columns stands *(43)*

SUNBURST a fanlike design *(26)*

SUPERPOSITION placing one order of columns over another *(49)*

SURROUND a decorative border or frame *(114, 132)*

SWAG a fabriclike decoration (also called a *festoon*) *(41)*

 SYRIAN ARCH an early-Christian *arch* rising from ground level *(94)*

THRESHOLD a doorsill; also the point of entry into a building

TIE BEAM a horizontal roof timber *(78)*

TRACERY curved *muntins* forming semicircular, triangular, and diamond-shaped patterns in glass or wood *(41)*

 TRANSOM LIGHT a horizonal set of small windows above a door *(22, 67)*

TREFOIL a cloverleaf pattern *(63)*

TRIGLYPH in classical architecture, a repeating trio of vertical lines *(37)*

TRUSS a triangular structural support composition *(78)*

TUDOR ARCH a flattened pointed arch *(62)*

TURNED WORK lengths of wood that are cut and shaped by being turned on a lathe, permitting circular forms and details *(82, 83)*

TURRET a slender corner tower

TYMPANUM the triangular area formed by a *pediment* *(30, 88)*

VERGEBOARD a wide board used to trim the edges of a *gable* (also called *bargeboard*) *(61)*

VIGA a wooden roof beam used in pueblo construction *(110)*

VOLUTE a spiral scroll design *(44, 82)*

WATER TABLE a *stringcourse* or other wall projection that throws off rainwater *(66)*

WATTLE a wall frame of woven branches or poles

WING WALL a low nonstructural wall extending out from a column *(94)*

 WROUGHT IRON iron rods and bars that are hammered or forged into shapes and designs *(115)*

REFERENCES

Books

Architects' Emergency Committee. *Great Georgian Houses of America*. Volume I. New York: Dover Publications, Inc., 1970.

Breeze, Carla. *American Art Deco*. New York: W. W. Norton & Company, 2003.

Framton, Kenneth, and Yukio Futagawa. *Modern Architecture 1920-1945*. New York: Rizzoli International Publications, 1983.

Girouard, Mark. *Sweetness and Light: The "Queen Anne" Movement, 1860-1900*. New York: The Clarendon Press, 1977.

Gowans, Alan. *Styles and Types of North American Architecture: Social Function and Cultural Expression*. New York: HarperCollins, 1992.

Grossman, Jill, and Curt Bruce. *Revelations of New England Architecture: People and Their Buildings*. New York: Grossman Publishers/The Viking Press, 1975.

Guild, Robin. *The Victorian House Book*. New York: Rizzoli International Publications, 1989.

Harris, Cyril M., ed. *Historic Architecture Sourcebook*. New York: McGraw-Hill, 1977.

Isham, Norman Morrison. *Early American Houses: The Seventeenth Century. 1928*. Watkins Glen, NY: Reprint, American Life Foundation, 1968.

Kennedy, Roger C. *Greek Revival America*. New York: A National Trust for Historic Preservation Book/Stewart Tabori & Chang, 1989.

Loth, Calder, and Julius Trousdale Sadler, Jr. *The Only Proper Style: Gothic Architecture in America*. Boston: New York Graphic Society/Little, Brown and Company, 1975.

McAlester, Virginia, and Lee McAlester. *A Field Guide to American Houses*. New York: Borzoi Books/Knopf, 1986.

Mullins, Lisa C., ed. *The Evolution of Colonial Architecture*. Pittstown, NJ: The National Historical Society/The Main Street Press, 1987.

Packard, Robert, and Balthazar Korab. *Encyclopedia of American Architecture*. New York: McGraw-Hill, 1980.

Pierson, William H., Jr. *American Buildings and Their Architects*. New York: Doubleday, 1970.

Poppeliers, John C. S.; Allen Chambers, Jr.; and Nancy B. Schwartz. *What Style Is It?: A Guide to American Architecture*. New York: Historic American Buildings Survey/John Wiley & Sons, Inc., 1983.

Scully, Vincent, Jr. *The Shingle Style and the Stick Style: Architectural Theory and Design from Richardson to the Origins of Wright*. New Haven: Yale University Press, 1955.

Whiffen, Marcus. *American Architecture Since 1780*. Cambridge, MA: The MIT Press, 1969.

Whiffen, Marcus, and Frederick Koeper. *American Architecture: 1607–1976*. Cambridge, MA: The MIT Press, 1981.

Web sites

www.about.com—architect, architecture

www.emporis.com

www.oldhouseweb.com

ACKNOWLEDGMENTS

Special thanks are due our literary agent, Jane Dystel of Dystel & Goderich, for her unflagging effort and support, and our inspired publisher and editor at Artisan—Ann Bramson and Ellice Eve Goldstein, respectively—who granted us ingress to this subject. Thanks also to Ted Mauseth at Mauseth Design, LLC, for the handsome jacket and layouts; Nick Caruso for his contributions to the jacket design; Vivian Ghazarian, Deborah Weiss Geline, Nancy Murray, Amy Corley, and Barbara Peragine.